"Kari is a powerful example that God will do amazing things in our lives—if we let him. God calls each of us to a bigger, greater life than we ever imagined, but only when we allow our stories to be part of God's great redemption story. Read this book and discover how God transformed the lives of one woman and her family when they sought to follow him."

RICHARD STEARNS, president of World Vision US and author of
The Hole in Our Gospel

"The temptation to divide life into the sacred and the mundane attacks most women every day of our lives. *Sacred Mundane* points out the heresy of this duality and provides hope that all of life can be valued as sacred. Kari is a mom in the trenches who wonderfully weaves strong theology with daily, down-to-earth application in an engaging and enjoyable way."

CHAUNDEL HOLLADAY, coauthor of *Love-Powered Parenting*

"Kari Patterson has a way with words, and oh how we need them! More than ever, voices all around tell us we need to dream big dreams and pursue big pursuits, but in *Sacred Mundane* Kari so beautifully reminds us that each of our days, if given their due, are quiet opportunities for a faith-filled life."

CHRISTINE HOOVER, author of *From Good to Grace*

"You had me with the title. *Sacred Mundane* stitches together vulnerable, nitty-gritty stories of life, offering practical lessons that inspire readers to seek after God's will—on their knees. Kari Patterson is as genuine and warm as every word in this delightful book, and she invites readers to share her journey to treasure every moment as monumental."

CORNELIA SEIGNEUR, Oregonian journalist and author of *WriterMom Tales*

"*Sacred Mundane* delivers a message that brings relief to women's souls—we are favored, loved, and chosen by the God of the universe. And as recipients of such favor, we have the awesome chance to draw closer to him each and every moment of our days. Kari's words, full of grace, humor, and practical application, invite us to transform the lens through which we see the world, through which we see God—through which we see everything."

JAMIE MARTIN, author of *Steady Days* and editor of the popular blogs
Simple Homeschool and *Steady Mom*

"Kari Patterson has written a book that all moms need to read. *Sacred Mundane* taps into our struggles and our pains, while offering us hope and strength to face each day with God's perspective. Our daily routine, with its mundane tasks and mindless repetition, is ultimately an offering of worship to God. What a great truth from a great God! Thanks, Kari, for enlightening all of us who struggle with the occasional drudgery of life and motherhood."

ANN BYLE, author of *The Making of a Christian Bestseller* and coauthor of *Devotions for the Soul Surfer*

"*Sacred Mundane* brings much-needed truth, hope, and inspiration for the weary woman's soul. For all of us entrenched in the mundane details of life, *Sacred Mundane* reads like a warm embrace, encouraging women to live whole lives of freedom, purpose, and joy. A must-read!"

ANGELA DAVIS, founder of the popular blog *Frugal Living NW*

"We want God to change us. Heal us. But like Naaman, we foolishly object to the *way* God wants to make us clean. This husband? These kids? This noisy, messy, sticky life? In *Sacred Mundane,* Kari Patterson—in her winsome, inspiring way—causes the muddy waters of daily life to actually seem inviting! For as we dip ourselves repeatedly into the things we wish we could change or escape or skip, these are the waters that God uses to make us clean and whole."

SHANNON POPKIN, author of *Control Girl*

Sacred MUNDANE

How to Find Freedom, Purpose, and Joy

KARI PATTERSON

Kregel
Publications

Sacred Mundane: How to Find Freedom, Purpose, and Joy
© 2017 by Kari Patterson

Published by Kregel Publications, a division of Kregel, Inc., 2450 Oak Industrial Dr. NE, Grand Rapids, MI 49505.

Published in association with the literary agency of Credo Communications, LLC, Grand Rapids, Michigan, www.CredoCommunications.net.

ISBN 978-0-8254-4447-0

2022-01

Printed in the United States of America

To my loves: Jeff, Dutch, and Heidi. You are my joy.

And to the countless everyday heroes who are faithfully, quietly, selflessly serving Jesus in the midst of the mundane. You are wiping counters, noses, bottoms. You are working dead-end jobs to provide for your family. You are making hard choices that no one sees or celebrates. You are silently saving souls through your tireless intercession. You hear no applause, receive little thanks, and too often go unnoticed. You are the heroes of heaven, of whom this world is not worthy. Thank you, faithful sisters and brothers. This book belongs to you.

There is not a square inch in the whole domain of our human existence over which Christ, who is Sovereign over all, does not cry: "Mine!"

—Abraham Kuyper

Contents

* · ◆ · *

Introduction: The Sentence of Your Life ➺→ 11

1 LET Him In ➺→ 19
2 LOOK: See the World Through the Word ➺→ 39
3 LISTEN: Discern His Voice in Daily Life ➺→ 59
4 ENGAGE: Enter In ➺→ 79
5 EMBRACE: Love the One ➺→ 97
6 TRUST: Live the Blank ➺→ 115
7 THANK: Find Fulfillment ➺→ 135
8 LET Your Life Be Poured Out ➺→ 159

Acknowledgments ➺→ 177
Small Group Bible Study: LET the Word
  Come to Life ➺→ 179
Notes ➺→ 211
About the Author ➺→ 213

The Sentence of Your Life

◆──────◆──────◆

He was a mighty man of valor, but he was a leper.
—2 Kings 5:1

GRAB A PENCIL. REALLY, go ahead. I know we've just met (hello!), but before we go much further I invite you to reflect on your life for just a moment. What you write will help us navigate the rest of our journey together, so please don't skip this part. Don't worry if it's not perfect; I said pencil on purpose. You can always erase and start over. Grace! But we have to start somewhere; let's try here.

If your life were a sentence, how would it read?

That is, if you simmered down your entire life into one short statement, just two clauses with a conjunction in the middle, what would it be?

While your wheels are beginning to turn, consider the short Scripture verse at the top of the page. This sentence describes Naaman, an oft-overlooked Old Testament character whose process of transformation will guide our own. There's a good chance your sentence will read a lot like his. You are a mighty man or woman of valor, you are a beloved child of God, *but* . . .

The whole verse reads, "Naaman, commander of the army of the king of Syria, was a great man with his master and in high favor, because by him the LORD had given victory to Syria. He was a mighty man of valor, *but he was a leper*" (2 Kings 5:1, emphasis mine).

Naaman had so much going for him. He was incredibly successful. He'd been used by God in a significant way. He was wealthy. Naaman's name comes from the Hebrew verb *naem*, meaning "to be pleasant, delightful, beautiful," which means he was probably handsome. He was "in high favor" with others, meaning he was popular and respected. He was in command, a powerful leader. But all of this was spoiled by the *but* in the sentence of his life. *But* . . . he was a leper, and leprosy cares nothing for Klout scores—it kills indiscriminately. This incurable disease would eventually steal it all, including Naaman's life. He would be unclean, isolated, rejected, shunned. His case is extreme, but it serves as an example for us all.

We all have a *but*, and it's a problem. (If you read that out loud it sounds terrible. I'm sorry; there was no other way.) Because you are created in the image of God, knit perfectly and wonderfully in your mother's womb and cherished by him, you have value and worth and honor. You are dazzling and delightful. You are dearly loved. You have gifts, talents, and innumerable things going for you. You have strengths and skills, power and potential.

❦

Hang-ups have a way of hijacking our identity.

But—there's something in the way. Something that limits our freedom, confuses our purpose, steals our joy. No matter what great things we have going for us, this thing constantly lurks on the fringe of our attention, subtly inhibiting, hindering, holding us back. For Naaman it was leprosy; for some it's crippling fear; for some it's anger or unforgiveness; for some it's a desperate need for approval; for some it's an issue or habit that's hung around so long it has become an accepted part of life. Hang-ups have a way of hijacking our identity. We wear the badge. It's who we are. *Naaman was a leper.*

Now, Naaman couldn't have carried on as commander with this issue out in the open; he had to hide it as long as he possibly could. We do the same. We wear long sleeves, so to speak. We know how to compensate for that weakness we've had with us for such a long time. We can still cope and manage life pretty well. Perhaps "it's no big deal," so we just shrug our shoulders and pretend it doesn't bother us. That much. But deep down we know there is something not quite right, something that subtly robs our peace and joy, something that clings to us and keeps us bound. Something we just can't kick.

And like leprosy, it spreads. Left alone, our hidden heartsickness always spreads. We think we're fine (we look fine!), sailing along in our long sleeves, but then that one thing—that person, that comment, that one hormonal moment—yanks off our protective layer, and we realize the problem is still there. It had been there all along, underneath. We resolve to deal with it. How? Add a turtleneck. Maybe some gloves. Don't get close to any situation where baring our skin or our souls is required. We become careful, cautious, learning to control our environment so our lack is less apparent.

But this isn't life. This isn't freedom. And we know it. Somewhere deep down, we know: this isn't the me I was created to be. This isn't the life I was meant to live.

If you identify at all, great. You're in good company. My hope is that we're all a bit fed up with this. My hope is that we'll finally say, "You know what? I've had it up to here with turtlenecks, and I'm sick of wearing gloves. I'm done with settling for surface solutions to my deep-down issues. I can't control this situation, and I hate feeling stuck. No matter what it takes, I want to be healed, I want to be whole, I want to be changed from the inside out. I want to be *free*."

If there is even a hint of that beautiful desperation in your heart, I'll take it. If you're fed up beyond words and sick to death of this blasted situation, that's even better. Desperation isn't a fun feeling, but it leads to transformation if we'll let it. See, change happens when the discomfort of our problem exceeds the discomfort of changing. Change is hard, but nothing is harder than living bound by our limitations and trying to convince ourselves that this is abundant life. Nothing is harder than living stuck.

This book is an invitation to live unstuck. To be healed, whole, changed from the inside out. To find freedom, purpose, and joy. In other words, it's an invitation to be transformed.

So, new friend, let's begin. What would be the *but* in the sentence of your life? Of course, there are probably quite a few. This definitely isn't a one-and-done sort of deal; in fact, it may take us a while to work through just the first half of our sentence. We need to know who we are before we can tackle what we're not. Don't worry, we'll work on that too. Just relax and write (in pencil) your initial sentence. There will be more, but we need one to begin with. God changes our lives one sentence at a time.

Now, here's the thing: we all long to see transformation—in our lives and in this world. But often we miss the most powerful catalyst for effecting true transformation in our lives: the dirty waters of daily life.

Often we miss the most powerful catalyst for effecting true transformation in our lives: the dirty waters of daily life.

See, Naaman was desperate for healing, so when he hears about the powerful prophet Elisha, he quickly speeds off in search of a supernatural encounter. He pulls out all the stops, loading his chariot with ten talents of silver, six thousand shekels of gold, and ten changes of clothes (2 Kings 5:5). Surely that will get him the finest treatment available. Pouring more money into a problem is often our first response; we think the result somehow depends on our own resources. We think we'll show God how serious we are by making our own elaborate plans and provisions.

Next, Naaman prepares himself for a grand encounter with the legendary prophet. What will it be like to see Elisha in person? Seeing this spiritual celebrity—that will surely bring the change Naaman desperately needs. He approaches Elisha's home. Here is the moment he's been waiting for. His heart pounds. His expectations soar. Will the transformation come through flashes of lightning? Thunder and a booming voice from heaven? Will it come through shouts and summoned power from on high? How will it happen? It will be something spectacular, to be sure! Some of you know the story: Elisha doesn't even bother to come out and meet him.

Excuuuse me? I can see Naaman, appalled. I know what he's thinking: *How dare Elisha not show up the way I wanted him to!*

Elisha sends word instead: "Go and wash in the Jordan seven times" (2 Kings 5:10). Naaman is livid. *What? In that dirty, smelly water? I thought my transformation would be more spectacular than this.*

Naaman is angry and goes away, saying, "'Behold, I thought that [Elisha] would surely come out to me and stand and call upon the name of the LORD his God, and wave his hand over the place and cure the leper. Are not Abana and Pharpar, the rivers of Damascus, better than all the waters of Israel? Could I not wash in them and be clean?' So he turned and went away in a rage" (2 Kings 5:11–12).

Forget it, Naaman says. *I quit.* He storms off, angry and disappointed.

Oh, friends, how often we want God to transform us on our terms! How often we think the answer to our problems is pouring out more money, getting more gear, seeing another spiritual celebrity, or seeking some spectacular experience. How often we balk at God's bidding when he tells us to simply go and dip down deep into what is right in front of us, the waters we most despise, because that is where true healing is found. How we wish for a prophet to wave his hand over us and miraculously make us mature, make us well, make us new. How we wish we could just walk through the doors of church and have the "godly dust" sprinkle down on us and make us whole. Can't we just get a spiritual spray-tan?

Truth: you are made new by dipping into the dirty, dusty dailiness of life. By letting your days transform your life.

It is the mundane, overlooked, ordinary stuff of life that changes us from the inside out. That heals us. That transforms us.

It is the sacred mundane that makes us new.

Friends, God has used this story countless times in my life. When I sobbed every Sunday after church because my son's behavior baffled me and I was embarrassed beyond words, God led me to Naaman and told me those humbling waters would heal my soul. Even today, every time I pitch a fit over some situation, God gently reminds me, "I love you. These are my waters of sanctification for you." How I've begged for my own waters and my own way! Yet in his infinite wisdom, God has chosen the waters right in front of me, and he quietly calls me to dip down into *here*.

Not surprisingly it is the servants of Naaman who talk some sense into the man. These lowly, humble folks who take care of the mundane tasks, they are the voice of reason: "My father, it is a great word the prophet has spoken to you; will you not do it?" (2 Kings 5:13).

This book is my humble plea: *Will you not do it?*

Will you not dip down deep into your dirty days and let God transform your life?

Thankfully, Naaman listened: "So he went down and dipped himself seven times in the Jordan, according to the word of the man of God" (v. 14).

I must interject here. Don't you love that Naaman had to dip seven times? Picture the scene. Here is esteemed, high-ranking, handsome, successful, powerful, popular Naaman, with all his gold and silver and chariots, gritting his teeth as he reluctantly goes down to the water and humbles himself by wading slowly in, deeper and deeper. He cannot go halfway. There's no way to go under the water without getting all the way wet. There's just no dignified way to do this. And after he finally swallows his pride and goes under once, he comes up and takes a breath, and the servants softly remind him, "Again."

Again. Oh yes. This is the sanctifying word of the sacred mundane. Often we hear the hard word, and we do the humbling thing, and then we get up the next morning, and wouldn't you know it—our loving Father says, "Again."

Again, again, again, again, again, again.

Over and over and over and over. Seven times Naaman had to dip until his pride was thoroughly washed away. Then we read the glorious ending: "And his flesh was restored like the flesh of a little child, and he was clean" (2 Kings 5:14).

No more did Naaman's sentence read, "but he was a leper." Now there was a new conclusion: "and he was clean."

The sentence of Naaman's life was forever changed.

How does God want to change the sentence of your life? I invite you to come, pencil in hand, and let the Good Author rewrite the broken fragments of your life. It's safe here. Not one of us has "arrived." We all have *buts*, but God wants us to be free. So, let's shed our turtlenecks, enjoy the fresh air, and get real about the stuff that's underneath. In the pages that follow I'll share my own Naaman story, my humbling, stumbling journey into the sacred mundane. We'll dip down deep into those dirty waters together and let our days transform our lives.

1

LET Him In

Behold, I stand at the door and knock. If anyone hears my voice and opens the door, I will come in to him and eat with him, and he with me.
—Revelation 3:20

It all began when I let her in. I remember those few moments quite clearly, like slow motion, not unlike the way an automobile accident victim recalls those split seconds before contact. Running into Penielle[1] was like a car crash for my comfort, and when I let her in that day, in that moment we made contact, my tidy little life careened out of control. I had no idea then how everything would change, how she would permeate every part of our home, our life. How we would never be the same again.

See, she had this slippery way of getting into everything. She filled every space. Years of addictive, abusive behaviors aren't immediately or easily unlearned. Boundaries, to her, were like low field fences to country children—made for climbing right over and running free, laughing all the way. But that wasn't the most unsettling part.

The part that messed with me was how I saw Jesus in her face. Her face that flashed with anger and twisted in pain and danced with laughter, all in one conversation. I knew what Mother Teresa had said about seeing Jesus in the face of the poor. But this? This infuriating and intoxicating presence that paraded into my home, into the everyday fabric of my life—could *this* be Jesus in disguise?

Could he be everywhere?

Unsettling. Letting her in was unsettling.

Letting Jesus in is unsettling too. I want to be clear, before we go further, that what we are about to embark on is unsettling. The world tells us we can add a dash of God here and there, a little religion or a splash of spirituality, like flavor for our lives. There are many, many varieties to choose from; we can pick what pleases our spiritual palette. But letting Jesus into your life, your real life, is absolutely nothing like salting your chicken. It's more like inviting a wrecking ball to dinner. In the most glorious way, Jesus messes with everything. He is an earthquake-ish sort of unsettling.

But—Jesus is so good and glorious and altogether lovely, life-giving, and life-changing that I guarantee you'll never regret letting him in. Everything he touches, he transforms. He brings hope, life, healing. He can turn every evil on its head and use it for our good. There is nothing else like what he does. He can redeem any relationship, heal any wound, calm any storm, part any sea, save any lost, and make masterpieces out of our worst messes. I guarantee you will never regret letting him into your life.

In my home, we have a wide variety of personalities. Most notably, we have my husband, Jeff, who is kind and capable and godly and wise, and who also happens to be the victim of an unfortunate genetic disorder that makes him incapable of being tidy. Really, it's a thing. It is probably just an unfortunate by-product of being a genius, but he cannot organize a physical space to save his life. He piles. He piles and piles and piles and piles. And I cry.

We've come a long way. I am an ordered, tidy person. I'm not as brilliant as Jeff, but I can find my car keys. We've worked things out over the past fourteen years, and our home is a happy mix of the order I crave and the relaxed imperfection he needs.

But there is one space Jeff won't let me in. His office. This room is a picture of what our life would be like if it were under his command alone, without the influence of his wife. It's terrifying. It is not good that man should be alone, people. However, we're currently in the process of moving, so my brilliant, godly, humble, wise husband has agreed it's time.

He'll let me in. Now, because I genuinely love him, I am going to honor his space. I'm not entering his space to shame him, poke fun, wag my finger, or shake my head in disgust. I fiercely love my man. He is the most godly, humble, gentle, kind, hardworking, faithful man I have ever met. I have committed my life to being the best helper I can possibly be to him. This means that when he lets me help, I will always act in a way that is for his good.

But it's going to be a mess. It's going to be unsettling. It's going to be dumping out drawers and sorting through piles and hauling mountains of garbage to the dump. It's going to mean things get worse before they get better. But if he'll trust me, I promise I can make things better for him. I'll do the hard work; I'm really good at this. I'll even teach him habits and tricks to help him become more organized going forward. I'll help him be all he was meant to be. I'm his helper—that's what I was made to do.

Did you know the same Hebrew word for "helper" that describes wives also describes God? He's our *ezer*. How fabulous is it that our job description is likened to God's!

There is a slight difference, of course, between God and me, but it's a good place to begin. He gives us an invitation to let him into our real lives, our ordinary, mundane lives. He stands at the door and knocks, patiently waiting to be invited in, knowing full well he can lovingly make something glorious out of our mess. Meanwhile we're often inside thinking we have to do it all on our own, wondering why we're stuck. We keep thinking we'll invite him over as soon as we have our lives tidied up a bit. Just a few more rounds of New Year's resolutions, then we'll be ready to have Jesus to tea. Certainly, he can't come over while we're still yelling at the kids and sipping wine from a mug.

Others of us have boarded up the windows and locked the doors because we've been given a tragically faulty view of God. We're terrified to let him in because we think he's the one behind the blow we've been dealt. We've gotten sovereignty terribly skewed and we think he hands out stuff like cancer for fun, that at any moment he might give us the gift of some horrific tragedy, so why would we want to get too close? Besides, if he hates gays and oppresses women and condones slavery, why would we want him in here? Not only that, we've probably *all* been wounded by his followers at some point. Won't the boss just be a bigger version of them? We have legitimate reasons for our reluctance to let God deeply into our lives.

Perhaps others of us aren't even home to invite God in because we think we must leave our ordinary, dreary mundanity behind to find something significant. Like Naaman, we substitute *spectacular* for *spiritual*, so we seek something *out there*. We're desperately looking for healing, wholeness, transformation, change. Some of us search in endless Christian conferences and some in shopping malls, but it's really all the same. We're all prodigals, out looking for abundant life, and the Father says, "Come home."

We're all prodigals, out looking for abundant life, and the Father says, "Come home."

The good Father is back at home—at our home—waiting. Jesus is knocking. And he is the greatest good, he gives the best gifts, his path is joy, his way is peace. He has precious and great promise-gifts that most of us haven't even begun to unwrap, and he's just waiting to be let into our ordinary days so he can make something more marvelous than we can imagine. This is good news, isn't it? All we have to do is go back home and let God into our lives. Our real lives. Our daily lives. The mundane.

The secret to true transformation isn't something to go find but Someone to let in.

WHO IS THIS?

My family and I currently live in the city with a bus stop at our front porch. Since a wide variety of interesting folks frequent the front of our house, and since I'm home with my littles all during the day, we always ask, "Who is it?" before opening the front door. In fact, we have often stood, frozen, my finger to my lips, waiting for some questionable character to quit knocking and leave.

We instinctively know we had better figure out who it is we're letting into our house. And if we're allowing someone in to *live* with us, we had better really figure out what exactly it will entail. We need to ask the following questions:

Who is this?

Where will she stay?

How long will she be here?

What will her role be in our home?

What are her expectations?

How will her presence change the environment?

Jeff and I wish we had asked these questions before letting Penielle (and others) in. And strangely enough, we wish Christians would ask these same questions when contemplating whether they will let Jesus come into their lives.

Whenever Jesus comes on the scene, the constant question is, "Who is this?" Matthew 21:10 tells us, "When [Jesus] entered Jerusalem, the whole city was stirred up, saying, 'Who is this?'" King David's prophetic poetry asked, centuries earlier, "Who is this King of glory?" (Ps. 24:10). Even Jesus himself, after hearing all the various opinions concerning his identity, pointedly questions his disciples, "But who do you say that I am?" (Matt. 16:15).

Before we can go on, we must answer this question ourselves: Who is this?

See, Jesus comes as King or nothing at all. This beautiful Savior, who stands at the door of our lives and knocks, is not our life coach, counselor, teacher, or daily dose of inspiration. He is not going to give us a new life by Friday. He loves us too much to give us a spiritual spray-tan. He will not be a quiet houseguest who keeps to his room and lets us peek our head in only to ask him for a pithy inspirational quote. Before we let him in, we must make the weighty decision to let him be everything he really is. As C. S. Lewis has famously said,

> You must make your choice. Either this man was, and is, the Son of God, or else a madman or something worse. You can shut him up for a fool, you can spit at him and kill him as a demon; or you can fall at his feet and call him Lord and God. But let us not come with any patronizing nonsense about His being a great human teacher. He has not left that open to us. He did not intend to.[2]

When the mighty leader of Israel, Joshua, saw an angel of the Lord, he asked the same question: Who is this? Joshua wisely wanted to know, "Are you for us, or for our adversaries?" But the angel responded, "No; but I am the commander of the army of the LORD. Now I have come." At this, Joshua "fell on his face to the earth and worshiped and said to him, 'What does my lord say to his servant?' And the commander of the LORD's army said to Joshua, 'Take off your sandals from your feet, for the place where you are standing is holy.' And Joshua did so" (Josh. 5:13–15).

I love this. Joshua asks if this person is for him or against him, and the angel responds: No. No, I am not "for you" in the sense that I fall in line with your own agenda. No, I am not "against you" in that I am seeking your demise. I am neither, because I am the authority. I am actually the One in charge.

Joshua rightly falls on his face in worship and immediately asks for his marching orders, submitting his will to the authority of God. Interestingly, what did God tell him to do? "Take off your sandals, Joshua, because where you are standing is holy."

When we invite God into our mundane, he's not for us or against us in this same sense. He is the commander. He is the authority. We bow our faces and take off our shoes and recognize this isn't our army. The holy is here. Here is the King of Kings and Lord of Lords, the Creator of heaven and earth, Yahweh, the Eternal God, the Alpha and the Omega, the Beginning and the End. In him all things that were made, were made. He holds all things together. He is the Almighty God and he is good. The end. This decision must be made: Will I let him in as Lord?

I know this is all really heavy right from the start. I wish we could begin differently. Actually, I don't. All good and glory and peace and freedom is found in falling on our faces to worship the one true God. It's really a waste of time to mess with anything else. Jesus won't ride shotgun. It's best we just go ahead and get out of the driver's seat and let him drive.

Let's not bother asking him to bless our lives until we will let him have our lives.

Let's not bother asking him to bless our lives until we will let him have our lives.

The quickest route to the glorious good he intends for us is to fall at his feet and recognize his matchless worth. Then, wonder of wonders, we will discover something absolutely amazing: doing life with Jesus is *awesome*. He is the coolest, funniest, smartest, most compassionate, powerful, life-giving, helpful, comforting, amazing person you could ever fathom. Actually, he's about a bazillion times better than we can imagine, and once we let him in, we get the eternity-long pleasure of getting to know this supremely wonderful Being.

When the nation of Israel was struggling and disobedient, God got fed up and told Moses they could go on ahead into the Promised Land—they could have the territory, the milk and honey—but he himself wouldn't be in their midst (Exod. 33:3). Moses's response will be ours if we have a lick of sense: "If your presence will not go with me, do not bring us up from here" (v. 15).

We need God's presence more than life itself. We need him more than a sentence changed, more than a problem fixed or even a disease healed. These are all glorious by-products of his power, but we need *him* most of all. And by his amazing grace, he offers himself to us freely. Jesus said, "If anyone loves me, he will keep my word, and my Father will love him, and we will come to him and make our home with him" (John 14:23).

Jesus comes to make his home in our hearts. In our lives. He openly acknowledges his intention of healing every hurt, binding up every wound, uprooting every idol, of cleansing and transforming our lives. He loves us exactly as we are, and far too much to let us stay stuck.

So, if we take the simple questions from earlier and ask them about Jesus, what do we find?

Who is this? Jesus Christ, the Son of God, King of Kings.

Where will he stay? Everywhere. He requires access to every room, every closet, every messy corner of our lives.

How long will he be here? Forever. He will never leave us or forsake us.

What will his role be in our home? Lord and Master. Lover and Friend.

What are his expectations? That we love and obey him.

How will his presence change the environment? Total transformation. He will make all things new.

I hope this clarifies who we're letting in. And just in case this Jesus-talk is a bit unfamiliar to you, I invite you to flip over to "The Gospel of Naaman" beginning on page 182. There you'll find more about this Jesus guy and the good news that he brings.

And so, I ask you: Will you let him in?

OUR SOLE OCCUPATION

No matter our gender, title, income, marital status, age, or stage of life, we all have the same job. Whoever or wherever we are, "Our sole occupation in life is to please God."[3] This is what we were created to do, in all things at all times. Ephesians 5:10 exhorts us to "find out what pleases the Lord" (NIV). So then, what pleases him?

Often we think of pursuing our own pleasure and passion as our own personal way of pleasing God. True, it is wonderful to experience a feeling of pleasure when we do what we love, and surely our Creator has wired us with certain inclinations and passions. However, feelings just aren't sufficient for determining something as important as how to fulfill our sole vocation in life. Thankfully, finding out for certain what pleases God is rather simple, and it just so happens to be the same thing you and I are currently seeking.

What pleases God? Transforming us. His will is our sanctification: "For this is the will of God, your sanctification" (1 Thess. 4:3). Sanctification is the Bible word for transformation. It describes the process of us becoming more like Jesus.

It is the will of God to change us from the inside out, to conform us to the image of his Son, to turn our lowly lives into glorious lives, to display his goodness for all the world to see. Our chief aim is to glorify God, and Jesus tells us exactly how this happens: "By this my Father is glorified, that you bear much fruit and so prove to be my disciples" (John 15:8).

God is pleased, God is glorified, God is happy
when our lives bear fruit.

God is pleased, God is glorified, God is happy when our lives bear fruit. And there's more good news: this can happen whether or not we travel to a foreign country, work in vocational ministry, get married, win a race, or have our name attached to some "great work" for God. Remember, the fruit to which Jesus is referring is *spiritual* fruit. You know, "The fruit of the Spirit is love, joy, peace, patience, kindness, goodness, faithfulness, gentleness, self-control; against such things there is no law" (Gal. 5:22–23).

Bearing fruit is what glorifies and pleases God, because the fruit of the Spirit are the things God is. Big buildings don't necessarily glorify God. Love does. Big followings don't necessarily glorify God. Faithfulness does.

God may choose to do spectacular things through your life, but first he must do spiritual things in your life.

Many people rise as great athletes, performers, pastors, and missionaries. They may have millions of fans and followers worldwide. They may please many. Yet those who please God are men and women who bear spiritual fruit, who reflect the character of God from the inside out. This can be done in the spotlight or the shadows, whether running for president or running water for a child's bath. If God's pleasure is our goal, then all of life becomes significant.

Every year, many "great" spiritual leaders fall away because of sin and selfishness, leaving an aftermath of thousands who are hurting, confused, and disillusioned with God. I have experienced it personally. We can no longer glorify "great works" more than godly character.

Scripture is clear: "Those who are in the flesh cannot please God" (Rom. 8:8). "But I say, walk by the Spirit, and you will not gratify the desires of the flesh" (Gal. 5:16). God is glorified when we bear spiritual fruit in our lives and so prove to be Jesus's disciples. He is pleased to make us look more and more like him.

He knows our "great works" will never give us lasting joy unless his great work, transformation, is done in our lives.

In short, God loves us so much that he wants us to be like him. He knows our greatest joy is found in knowing, loving, and becoming like him. He knows *our* "great works" will never give us lasting joy unless *his* great work, transformation, is done in our lives. Outward successes will never satisfy unless sanctification accompanies, deep within our souls. Because of his extraordinary love, God goes to great lengths to woo us and win our hearts, to work his way through our lives so that no dark corners keep us bound in shame. Relentlessly, graciously, he moves through every mundane moment of our lives, using all that is ordinary to transform us into glory. He replaces bondage with freedom, apathy with purpose, despondency with joy. All in the midst of our regular routines. This is what pleases God.

MATERIAL FOR SACRIFICE

Let's back up for a bit and look at how this sacred mundane thing began. At twenty years old, I was on fire for God. I was eager to devote my life to sacred work. Inspired by William Carey, I wanted to expect great things from God and attempt great things for God. I plunged headlong into the sacred waters of church work, attending a ministry training school, traveling and leading overseas mission trips, teaching classes, leading Bible studies, writing gospel dramas, discipling college women, you name it. There was only one problem.

I was miserable.

I wanted to please God, but the reality was that life was about 2 percent holy high and 98 percent ordinary, irritating, boring stuff. Nothing I hoped for was coming to pass. The man I loved did not love me. My thriving "ministry" mostly included a lot of toilet scrubbing, taking out the trash at church, and late-night, long hours spent with people who drained me dry. On the outside, I might have looked fine, but deep down I saw no eternal purpose in much of what my job entailed. I longed to be free from my tendency to turn to food for comfort. I found myself slipping more and more into depression, wondering what happened to my joy. I desperately wanted *a* change and wanted *to* change. But I didn't know how.

I don't even remember what specific straw broke the proverbial camel's back, but one morning another mundane day stretched out excruciatingly ordinary before me and I just couldn't get out of bed. As minutes turned to hours I finally told myself what I told everyone else: trust God and do the next thing.

I pulled my Bible from the nightstand and flipped to find the brown ribbon that marked the place for my daily reading. My eyes fell on

Leviticus 5. *Awesome. I'm in Leviticus. Discharges and nakedness. This will be inspiring.*

Paying half attention, I began to read: "If anyone touches . . . a carcass of an unclean wild animal . . . or a carcass of unclean swarming things . . ."

That did it. *Seriously? Lord, please. Carcasses of swarming things? For crying out loud! My heart is broken, I'm dying inside, and this is all you have to say?*

I almost put the Bible down, but turned the page instead and began chapter six. A dozen verses later, my gracious God whispered through his Word: "The fire on the altar shall be kept burning on it; it shall not go out. The priest shall burn wood on it every morning. . . . Fire shall be kept burning on the altar continually; it shall not go out" (Lev. 6:12–13).

The fire shall always be kept burning. It shall not go out. With the clarity, if not the volume, of an audible voice, I heard: I am giving you material for sacrifice.

Material for sacrifice.

I truly wanted to live a life that pleased God, that glorified God. Yet I found my life was full of pain. It was full of ordinary days. It was full of disappointment. It was full of toilet scrubbing and trash toting. How was I to glorify God with that?

Material for sacrifice. The fire on the altar shall be kept burning.

It didn't all make sense just then, but as I peered at those words in the most mundane of Bible books, I saw that God was giving me a wide variety of things—hopes, dreams, longings, ideas, routine tasks, ordinary days, even pain—opportunities for me to offer them back up to him as a sacrifice of praise.

Every dream yet unfulfilled: sacrifice material.

Every tedious task: sacrifice material.

Every frustrated plan: sacrifice material.

Every hurt and rejection: sacrifice material.

At the time, this revelation was enough, but later I would look it all up. What is a sacrifice anyway? The word *sacrifice* comes from the Latin *sacrificus*, from *sacra*, meaning "sacred," and *facere*, meaning "to do, to perform." Our English word *sacrifice* literally means "sacred doing" or "sacred performing." In Hebrew (stick with me here), the word for "sacrifice" in these Leviticus passages is *korban*, which comes from a root that means "to come close." In other words, a *korban* is a vehicle for mankind to come close to God.

A sacrifice, then, is the sacred act of offering something to God for the purpose of drawing near to him. Our days, our pain, our dreams, our bodies, our lives—offered up to God for the purpose of drawing near. Sacrifice material. All of life, a sacred offering.

But wait—what about Jesus? Isn't he the true sacrifice, offered once and for all so we no longer have to offer sacrifices? Isn't all that Old Testament altar stuff done and gone? We don't have to sacrifice anymore, right? Hebrews 13:15–16 explains, "Through [Jesus] then let us continually offer up a sacrifice of praise to God, that is, the fruit of lips that acknowledge his name. Do not neglect to do good and to share what you have, for such sacrifices are pleasing to God." Isn't this awesome? Because of Jesus's once-and-for-all atoning sacrifice (removing all guilt for our past, present, and future sin) we may freely and joyfully approach the throne of God and offer our ongoing, living sacrifice of praise.

The sacrifice of atonement was Jesus's work; the sacrifice of praise is ours. It's through his sacrifice that we offer ours. We are positionally pleasing to God because of Christ's sacrifice; we are practically pleasing to God because of ours.

———— ❧ ————

The sacrifice of atonement was Jesus's work; the sacrifice of praise is ours.

This sacrifice of praise that pleases God involves the ordinary, mundane tasks we do each day. The taking of every moment and continually offering it up in worship.

Romans 12:1 says the same thing: "I appeal to you therefore, brothers, by the mercies of God, to present your bodies as a living sacrifice, holy and acceptable to God, which is your spiritual worship."

My life, a "living sacrifice," is intended to be a continual act of praise. That is what it means to glorify God, please God, and enjoy God, entering each moment as a sacred place of worship and letting him transform me in the process.

Brother Lawrence said the same thing: "Sanctification does not involve changing what we do, but in doing our normal activities for God's sake."[4] We are transformed as we worship God through our ordinary days. True worship isn't a song we sing; it's a life we live. It's a sacrifice. A continual offering.

> True worship isn't a song we sing;
> it's a life we live.

This is how the mundane becomes sacred. We hallow it. To "hallow" means to "make holy." When we set about our unspectacular days with the express purpose of offering everything up as a sacrifice of praise, we make holy the ordinary. John Keble said it this way in his hymn:

> If on our daily course our mind
> Be set, to hallow all we find,
> New treasures still, of countless price,
> God will provide for sacrifice.

If we set our minds to make holy all that we find, God will provide treasures, plenty of material for sacrifice, and limitless opportunities for worship.

Back in my room, I looked up from Leviticus and out the window at the parking lot full of cars, the garbage bins, the bicycles. Could this mean that all of life was sacred? Was it possible to enter every moment as a sacrifice of praise? To offer all to God? To let him use everything to make me more like him?

I looked back at the ordinary words resting on the page. I had no idea how this truth would grow to touch every fiber of my being. But this, I knew, would be the foundation for the rest of my days. I found in my desk a tiny blank notebook, opened to the first page, and with trembling hand, wrote in pen the manifesto of my life:

sacred mundane

HUPOMONE

Now that we've covered the backstory, let's get busy. The rest of our time together involves practice. I believe God has given us some mind-blowing truths and insights and wisdom from his Word, and I can't wait to share more of my ongoing, humbling-fumbling journey learning this stuff. But please promise me you will practice each step we take. Deal? This'll only work if you do! Let's agree to let our days transform our lives.

How exactly? LET. We must grasp this glorious truth: LET is the key.

James 1:4 reads, "*Let* steadfastness have its full effect, that you may be perfect and complete, lacking in nothing" (emphasis mine). This is what we need, right? To be perfect and complete, lacking nothing. Yes, please! But interestingly, we become perfect and complete not by going out and doing something but by letting something happen to us. And yet, this letting is not entirely passive.

True, to surrender is to let go of something, but if you have ever surrendered something you know the doing so is anything but passive! It is usually a knock-down, drag-out battle against our flesh to say no to ourselves and surrender something to God. Similarly, to *let* something happen implies passivity, but this is focused effort if ever there was—to engage in the daily battle of letting steadfastness have its work in my life.

How do we let steadfastness have its full effect? Well, it is with great joy that I introduce you to one of my favorite words in all the world. Are you ready? *Hupomone.* Isn't that great? *Hupomone* is the Greek word for "steadfastness" in James 1:4. Also translated "endurance," it is mentioned thirty-one times in the New Testament and is one of the best words in Scripture, hands down.

Hupomone does not mean just sitting, head down, and enduring something (the way many of us joylessly endure life's dull duties). Instead, it means

> not only the ability to bear things, but the ability, in bearing them, to turn them into glory. It is conquering endurance. *Hupomone* is the spirit which no circumstance in life can ever defeat and no event can ever vanquish. *Hupomone* is the ability to deal triumphantly with anything that life can do to us.[5]

Go ahead and read that again.

Amen! This is what I want in my life, don't you?

So, how do we get us some *hupomone*? We're gonna need a double dose. How we get *hupomone* is clearly outlined in Romans 5:3–4: "We rejoice in our sufferings, knowing that suffering produces endurance, and endurance produces character, and character produces hope."

This is the process of transformation—when we *let* the ordinary inconveniences (sufferings) of daily life produce *hupomone* in us, changing our character from the inside out (spiritual fruit) and birthing hope in our hearts. See, every time we face a crisis and choose to believe, endure, and see God come through, our faith grows and we're more able to endure the next crisis. We become more Christlike in our character and our hope is drastically increased because we've proven God's faithfulness that much more. Each time God meets us, greater hope is birthed. Walking with Jesus should make us the most hopeful, joy-filled people in the world!

The dirty waters of daily life, the everyday muck we'd rather avoid, are exactly where this *hupomone* is produced. Sure, these things may not be "suffering" in the same sense as a death or disease, but they are the mini sufferings of daily life, the kind we most often encounter. All these mini sufferings produce the endurance we will need when we inevitably face far greater challenges down the road.

These small, daily sufferings work for us; 2 Corinthians 4:17 makes this clear: "Our present troubles are small and won't last very long. Yet they produce for us a glory that vastly outweighs them and will last forever!" (NLT, emphasis mine). Other translations say "work" for us, or "achieve" for us, or "prepare" for us. It doesn't get much clearer: all those little inconveniences you're facing today are working for you. How so? By building spiritual strength. By producing *hupomone* in your life.

Hupomone is produced spiritually the same way muscles are produced physically. Now, friends, common sense tells us it is easier to lift our arms overhead when we're not holding anything in our hands. (I told you I wasn't brilliant, but I know this as fact.) Why in the name of all that is good would we put heavy things in our hands and lift them overhead, especially in reps of ten or twenty, and especially until we feel pain in our arms? Some of us even pay money to do this! Why would we choose to "feel the burn" and pursue a more painful path?

Hupomone is produced spiritually the same way muscles are produced physically.

Glory. Glory lures us on. We want the glory of strong muscles, health, a fit body. We're after the glory of victory, no matter how small. Most days I'm just after the glory of a clean house. The simple glory of a fresh cup of coffee lures me out of bed every morning.

We were made for glory. God created us with a hunger for glory, and that very hunger is glorious! Everyone seeks glory, but it is the kind of glory we're after that distinguishes us. The world wants physical, visible, temporal glory. We, as Christ followers, see differently and seek differently. "This light momentary affliction is preparing for us an eternal weight of glory beyond all comparison, as we look not to the things that are seen but to the things that are unseen. For the things that are seen are transient, but the things that are unseen are eternal" (2 Cor. 4:17–18).

As believers who have the mind of Christ, we see this world with a completely different lens than unbelievers. We see the eternal. We see the unseen. We see that the sufferings here on earth are simply hand weights for our spiritual workout. They strengthen our faith, sharpen our discernment, deepen our character, increase our hope. Sometimes life hands us two-pound weights, and we skate through the day fairly easily. Sometimes the weights feel unbearable, and our shaking, trembling faith muscles are burning. We desperately want to quit.

But transformation is taking place. Just as our bodies are transformed through physical exercise, our lives are transformed through spiritual exercise. Through the testing of our faith. Remember James 1:4? How we let *hupomone* have its work in us? The sentence preceding says this, "Consider it all joy, my brethren, when you encounter various trials, knowing that the testing of your faith produces endurance" (vv. 2–3 NASB). You already know what the biblical Greek word for "endurance" is there, right? *Hupomone!* There it is! *Hupomone* is produced how? By the testing of our faith. By the hand weights handed to us. Daily.

The only way to honestly "consider it all joy" when we encounter trials is to know that these trials are producing glory for us.

Why is this so important? Why belabor the point about suffering producing endurance? Because if it weren't for the hope of glory, none of those exercisers would grab hand weights at all. If I didn't believe exercise is good for me, I would never endure the pain. The only way to honestly "consider it all joy" when we encounter trials is to know that these trials are producing glory for us.

This is what pushes us through the pain when we don't feel strong. The process of strengthening our muscles actually involves them being torn down, weakened by exercise, then allowing them to heal, and through the process they are made stronger than before. My arms never feel strong when I'm hefting hand weights overhead for the hundredth time; they feel exactly the opposite. But in this weakness, this tearing down, healing will happen and greater strength will arise. This gives me the hope to push through the pain, trusting the process, looking toward the goal: Glory. Spiritual strength. *Hupomone.*

Our ordinary days, filled with tedious tasks and frequent frustrations, are working for us. When we *let* Jesus in and let all things produce spiritual strength in our lives, we live mysteriously powerful lives of peace and joy. We live as more than conquerors. We live unruffled and unfazed, and we offer this unshakable peace and joy to a desperate world in the name of Jesus Christ.

This is how we *let* our days transform our lives. We let him in and offer up everything as material for sacrifice on the altar of our lives, letting Christ use the dirty waters of daily life to heal us, strengthen us, and make us whole. Practically speaking, how do we do this? Stick with me. In the next six chapters, we will use this key word, LET, as a guide, leading us through a six-step process of learning to do exactly this.

We will LOOK, LISTEN, ENGAGE, EMBRACE, TRUST, and THANK. We will dip down into our days and LET him change the sentence of our lives. Let's go ahead and step into the sacred mundane.

2

LOOK: See the World Through the Word

Without God's Word as a lens, the world warps.
—Ann Voskamp, *One Thousand Gifts*

I ONLY WORE THE drunk goggles once, but it was enough. I've never forgotten their lesson. Technically they're called *alcohol impairment simulation goggles*, a teaching tool used to illustrate the effects of intoxication. Every September, as college freshmen flocked to our college campus, the police department set up a booth, offering a considerable prize to anyone who could walk a straight line while wearing the warped lenses. Of course, overconfident youth lined up dozens deep, eager to prove their ability to remain unaffected by the distortion and win a prize in front of their peers.

No one could. We all took turns trying them on, laughing hysterically at each other as we tried to walk a straight line while impaired. Inevitably we each stumbled, or tripped, or leaned so heavily in one direction, we wound up falling down altogether. It was uncanny, really, how a simple thing like visual impairment could affect even our ability to stand up straight. I couldn't perform the simplest task while wearing the distorted lenses, let alone navigate other obstacles. If I had had to face physical challenges—say, climbing stairs or jumping hurdles—I'd have failed for sure.

I don't know whether or not the goggles kept students from consuming alcohol, but they impressed me with a foundational truth I'll never forget: if we can't see clearly, we fall.

Now, imagine attempting to *live* while wearing these drunk goggles. Imagine trying to type, drive, run, swim. We'd be misstepping and crashing and falling and drowning! We'd never survive.

If we can't see clearly, we fall.

Further, imagine if these drunk goggles equally impaired our minds. Our emotions. Our behavior. Our decisions. Imagine if all of life, every action and relationship and spoken word, were filtered through a tragically flawed lens. Imagine if we lived looking at every aspect of life through this severely skewed perspective. Imagine if this distortion even extended to how we viewed ourselves—and how we viewed God. The result would be disastrous, yes?

Many precious people, created in the image of God for purpose and beauty and glory, are stumbling around spiritually, crashing and falling, drowning in deception, lost in this labyrinth of life, desperate for direction but unable to see. We may have perfectly presentable lives on the outside, we may have success and tidy homes, we may have kids with manners, a decent marriage, maybe even a 401(k). But something's skewed ever so slightly, and the result is dizzying and disillusioning. We want to see clearly, but our default is drunk goggles and we don't even know we're wearing them. We battle a subtle sense of hopelessness, or wonder why nothing seems to satisfy as it should. We throw ourselves into one peripheral thing after another, driven by a gnawing discontentment. We scan social media, looking for something. Anything. We pray for one thing and the exact opposite seems to happen, and in honest moments we're not quite sure any of this Christianity stuff really works, but of course we can't say that out loud. So, we go to church, smile, sing, sip coffee, and hear another sermon, then return to real life, where exactly nothing has changed.

Perhaps we have a vague sense of guilt over not reading our Bibles and praying like we should, or not giving more to orphans in Africa, or not volunteering in the nursery at church, but the truth is we're just trying to keep the wheels on. Sometimes, in quiet moments, we sense we were made for something more, that there might actually be greatness bundled up deep down somewhere. But life feels overwhelmingly complex, and there's barely enough energy to clean the bathroom, let alone tackle something like human trafficking. By the time dinner dishes are done it's just so much easier to flip on the TV and tune out. Greatness can wait.

No matter who you are, whether you have walked with Jesus five minutes or fifty-five years, we all have one thing in common: we need to see more clearly. Nothing matters more. No amount of practical instruction will do us a lick of good if we're seeing everything through distortion. This is why we need the Word of God. We must see the world through the Word.

In our desire for transformation, we'll never succeed if we begin by addressing our behavior. We must begin with belief. All behavior stems from belief: we always act according to what we believe. Always. Every single person on earth is a believer. Not everyone believes in Jesus, but everyone believes. When you drive through a green light, it's because you believe the other light (which you cannot see) is red and therefore the cross traffic will stop. You purchase an item because you believe it is worth the price. You exercise (or don't) because you believe (or don't) in its benefits. We always act according to what we believe. All errant behavior is a result of errant belief. If we see an area in our life where our behavior has gotten off track, guaranteed it's because our belief has gotten off track. Something's off with our beliefs, with our minds. We see something askew.

Can we just honestly admit that we all most likely believe something that's false? I've yet to meet someone who honestly believed she was one-hundred-percent spot-on in her view of life. But here's the tricky part: What do you believe that's false?

Crickets. Right? Because we don't know. It's impossible to know what we believe that's false, because we believe it. If we didn't believe it, we wouldn't believe it! (Have I confused you yet?) We actually believe it, therefore there's no way for us to unbelieve it to see that we shouldn't believe it. This creates a problem. What else can we do but throw up our hands and succumb to our sad state of self-deception?

There's good news. There is a way to take off the drunk goggles and see clearly. There is a way to identify where our belief has gotten off track. Think of it this way: Have you ever wondered if something is navy blue or black? It's nearly impossible to tell sometimes if you just hold it up by itself, so what do you do? You hold it up next to something you know. You hold it up to the shirt that you know is black. Only then can you see the difference.

This is exactly what we do with the Word of God. We hold up our lives, as honestly as we can, and compare our thoughts and emotions and behaviors to the truth of the Scriptures. The Bible is the only thing we know to be true, to be completely pure and clear, without distortion. No other book or person, no matter how popular or respected, will work as the "black shirt" by which we detect error. Only when we hold up our lives next to the perfect truth can we see the difference.

The Bible is the only thing we know to be true, to be completely pure and clear, without distortion.

The only way to take off the drunk goggles is to look instead through the crystal clear, perfect perspective of God's holy Word. See, every single day we are handed the drunk goggles. We don't even have to look hard to find them. I find that I wake up wearing them (argh!). It doesn't seem fair that drunk goggles are the default, but they are, and shedding them is the secret to true transformation.

Scripture tells us not to be conformed to this world (Rom. 12:2). The world around us is constantly pressing us into its mold, telling us what to think, how to look, and what to want. It's feeding us its flawed perspective every single day. But the Bible is clear: don't be conformed. Don't let the world slip those drunk goggles over your eyes and make you stagger and stumble. Lift up the Word of God and look *through it* to see clearly, to keep from falling.

The rest of that verse reads, "But be transformed by the renewal of your mind." How does transformation happen? By a renewed mind; we refuse the distortion and choose instead to renew our minds daily by the truth of God's Word. Only then will we see clearly and know God's good and perfect will. Only then will the sentences of our lives begin to change.

Just months after trying on those drunk goggles, I stumbled upon a simple practice that has proved to be the most powerful catalyst for spiritual transformation. Though I had grown up in a healthy Christian home, I had never regularly read my Bible. I knew stories, had a general understanding of the gospel, and loved lighthearted devotionals that gave me an uplifting verse for the day, but I had never made a regular habit of Scripture reading.

Then I met Anne Ortlund. In her classic book, *Disciplines of a Beautiful Woman*, she offhandedly mentions that she reads through the Bible every year. Simple. Four chapters a day did the trick. I still remember sitting in my dorm room, as if time stood still. Though I'd never regularly read my Bible, the simplicity of reading through it, cover to cover, each year, made so much sense! Suddenly it seemed very doable. I realized that if God gave me even eighty years of life, I could read through the Bible more than sixty times. If I was blessed with long life, I could quite possibly read it seventy-five times! I began, hungrily, that day.

Now, as I near twenty times reading through the Bible, I can honestly say that other than my choice to trust Christ for salvation, this one simple decision has transformed my life more than any other. Just thirty minutes a day keeps me from staggering through life with the drunk goggles and keeps me walking strong and steadfast, by God's grace.

If the only takeaway you get from this book is a renewed hunger for God's Word and a resolve to read it regularly, that alone would make the writing worth it to me. These words I'm writing are nothing in comparison to his holy, perfect, life-changing, heart-transforming words. Only his words can change you from the inside out.

❧

For the first few years, I came each day to the Scriptures just looking for encouragement. A meaningful verse. A pithy quote. A quick pick-me-up. Since I was a baby in my faith, this was a good place to begin—at least my Bible was open! Years later I went to ministry school and seminary, where I took many courses on how to interpret the Bible. I loved it. I am a Bible teacher at heart and could easily digress and wax eloquent about lexical-syntactical analysis and chiastic structure. I won't. I am grateful for glorious hermeneutical scholarship, but for the part of life where we *live*, I suggest another method. Instead of using my life to interpret the Word, what if I used the Word to interpret my life? Instead of asking, How do I interpret the Bible? what if we asked, How does the Bible interpret me?

> Instead of using my life to interpret the Word,
> what if I used the Word to interpret my life?

I suggest to you this simple approach to the Scriptures: first *receive* it, then *look through* it at everything else. See the world through the Word. Don't just study the Bible; let the Bible study you.

When we merely "do Bible study," we hold ourselves over the Bible, scrutinizing it and holding our own life experiences above it. We begin sharing "what it means to me." We can claim a "high view of Scripture" and still shamelessly manhandle its contents to make it say what we want. Please, it is impossible to overstate how susceptible we are to reading the Scriptures through the distorted lens of our own limited experience. We read that Jesus healed every person who came to him, but we've never personally seen someone supernaturally healed, so God must not still heal today. We read that Jesus calls us to love our enemies, but we're quick to explain why our situation is different. We read God's clear design for sexuality and marriage, "but we love each other" so it must be okay. We are constantly tempted to lower the Scriptures to match our lives, rather than asking God to raise our lives to match his Word.

The truth is, it's terribly uncomfortable to admit how much of the Bible seems completely foreign to our lives. It bothers me. It should. Here's a freeing truth: it's okay to be bothered. Let's go further: it's good to be bothered. One more step: we should be bothered!

That's just it: the Bible bothers us in the best way. The Bible confronts me in a way that nothing else can. I can quite easily surround myself with blogs, magazines, shows, and books that all affirm what I already believe. We all do it. Even Facebook is designed to surround us with what we already "like." We're naturally drawn toward what will affirm how we already live and what we already think. This is why we're susceptible to self-deception, to those drunk goggles that leave us stumbling through life. We can easily insulate ourselves from anything that contradicts our own treasured truths.

But the Bible won't bow to us. It won't support our self-deception, because God loves us too much to let us live that way. His Word is the only thing powerful enough to remove the drunk goggles and allow us to see clearly. Through his Word we see ourselves rightly, we see his love rightly, we see the world rightly. Only through his Word can we know how to truly love others, how to live wisely, how to walk in wholeness.

Christians are famous for "shoulding" people. You should read your Bible. You should pray. You should give. These things are true, but a closer look at the Scriptures reveals something drastically different: we're crazy not to! We're crazy not to hold up the perfect, clear lens of God's Word so we can see clearly, live wisely, and let our lives be transformed from the inside out.

Of all the people I saw trying on the drunk goggles, not a single person chose to keep them on the rest of the day. No one. Every single person chose to take them off. Not because others of us begged them to or told them they should. They took them off because anyone in his right mind wants to see clearly. I'm guessing you do too, and I invite you to do just that.

How? The first step: receive.

AN INVITATION: RECEIVE

Only in the last five hundred years have English Bibles been widely accessible. For almost all of human history the Word of God was not read. It was received. In fact, notice how Scripture intake is described within its pages. In the Old Testament a father exhorts his son, *"Receive* my words and treasure up my commandments with you" (Prov. 2:1, emphasis mine). The prophet Jeremiah implores God's people, "Let your ear receive the word of [God's] mouth" (Jer. 9:20), and Ezekiel commands, "All my words that I shall speak to you receive in your heart" (Ezek. 3:10).

Jesus says in prayer to the Father, "I have given them the words that you gave me, and they have received them" (John 17:8). Throughout Acts the early church is established as people receive the Word of God: "Those who received his word were baptized, and there were added that day about three thousand souls" (2:41); "Samaria had received the word of God" (8:14); "The Gentiles also had received the word of God" (11:1).

Paul commends the Thessalonians, saying, "You became imitators of us and of the Lord, for you received the word in much affliction, with the joy of the Holy Spirit" (1 Thess. 1:6). He continues, "We also thank God constantly for this, that when you received the word of God, which you heard from us, you accepted it not as the word of men but as what it really is, the word of God, which is at work in you believers" (2:13).

James is also clear: "Put away all filthiness and rampant wickedness and receive with meekness the implanted word, which is able to save your souls" (James 1:21). Solomon, Jeremiah, Ezekiel, Jesus, Luke, Paul, James—all speak of *receiving* the word of truth. Perhaps the best example for us is the noble Bereans: "They received the word with all eagerness, examining the Scriptures daily to see if these things were so" (Acts 17:11).

They not only received; they also *examined*. That is, they used the Word as a lens to see the world. They used the Word as a filter for everything that came their way. Remember, these Bereans were hearing New Testament "Scripture" (Paul's words) but didn't know it was Scripture. This gospel message was new and foreign to their way of thinking. And what did they do? They compared the truth of what they knew to be God's Word, the Old Testament, with these new claims to prove whether they were true. They had already received the Old Testament Scriptures, so they were able to discern that these new teachings were in fact truth.

The same is true for us. Thankfully, we have a much fuller revelation of God's Word than the Bereans did. We have the whole counsel of God, revealed to us in the Old and New Testaments. When we receive his Word, we submit to it, study it, and seek to more fully understand it so we can become skillful at holding it up as our lens. Then we are able to examine every new claim or circumstance that comes our way, wisely discerning what lines up with the absolute truth of God's Word.

———— ❧ ————

When we receive his Word, we submit to it, study it, and seek to more fully understand it so we can become skillful at holding it up as our lens.

Receiving the Word doesn't mean we turn off our brains, but it does mean we turn off our egos. James said we are to receive the Word with meekness. It takes humility to receive rather than merely read. When we think of reading something we think of entertaining new ideas, holding things up and turning them over in our minds, critiquing them and judging them to see what we think. So, when we *read* the Word we approach it in that way—giving ourselves the final say on whether a truth is allowed to carry weight in our lives or not. On the other hand, when we *receive* the Word, we let it say whatever it wants to us. We bow. We open the Word on our knees and allow it to take root in us. Dietrich Bonhoeffer said it like this: "It is not necessary that we should discover new ideas in our meditation [on the Word]. Often this only diverts us and feeds our vanity. It is sufficient if the Word, as we read and understand it, penetrates and dwells within us. . . . [Then] it strives to stir us, to work and operate in us, so that we shall not get away from it the whole day long. Then it will do its work in us, often without our being conscious of it."[1]

Each morning we receive the Word like a pair of glasses that enable us to see clearly all day long. We open ourselves up to the Word of God and it, in turn, works in us and allows us to see all things through its lens. It interprets our days. *He* interprets our days.

This is how we gain understanding and spiritual insight. While I am deeply grateful for my years of seminary study, I can honestly say my most life-changing encounters with the Scriptures have happened in the quiet of my own room, alone with the Lord, allowing his Word to speak to the hidden places of my heart. We needn't worry about our intellectual limitations or our inability to grasp lofty concepts. We don't need a certain IQ to know God. Jesus loved to hide things from scholars and show them to kids.

The bottom line is this: our aptitude for God's Word matters so much less than our attitude toward God's Word. The most important thing is how we approach his Word: With pride or with meekness? Reading or receiving? Merely hearing or doing as well? I have prayed much over this chapter and asked God to reveal his heart for us concerning his Word. The one thing that has been impressed on my heart again and again is this: do not let what you don't understand keep you from applying what you do understand.

As Mark Twain wryly stated, "It ain't those parts of the Bible that I can't understand that bother me, it is the parts that I do understand." Oh, that we'd be so concerned about the parts we understand that we'd quit worrying about all that we don't.

Just this morning I soaked in the gospel of Luke. There was much in it that I didn't understand, specifically about the end times. After going over it a few times, wondering about "those who are in Judea fleeing into the wilderness," about "Jerusalem trampled underfoot," about "signs in the sun and moon and stars," I stopped and prayed. *Father, what do you want me to know about this passage?* As I waited in silence, the clear statement echoed in my heart: *This is not a game.*

Immediately I knew what that meant. This, this Christian life, this is not a game. Following Christ isn't a hobby. Jesus is coming back. Are we all in?

Please note that I am not advocating some secret interpretation of Scripture. What echoed in my heart is absolutely harmonious with the rest of God's Word. I had simply asked God to show me how he wanted me to use this passage as an interpretation for my day.

Today I will take this one small passage about end times and hold it up and know that this sacred life is not a game. I will look at my day with a sacred seriousness that adds weight to my actions. I will discipline my children with diligence because this is not a game. I will be mindful of my habits, how I spend my time, because this is not a game. I will seek him earnestly throughout the day because this is not a game. I won't dabble in disobedience because this is not a game.

Do you see how the Word interprets our days? Even small portions of Scripture can interpret large portions of life.

Even small portions of Scripture can interpret large portions of life.

If you know even one verse, you can obey that verse and memorize that verse and ask yourself, *What does this verse tell me about God?* Then ask him, *What do you want me to know about this verse?* And then hold up that verse and look through it every single day and let it interpret the world for you. Let it be your lens. Let your world come into focus based on what that verse tells you. Sometimes we're frantically doing so many Bible studies and listening to so many podcasts that we get too many verses rattling around in our brains, and we're not receiving any of them. Jesus said, "Be careful how you hear," and James exhorts us to be "doers of the Word." Let's not move on to "learn" more until we obey what we already know. Whatever it is that you've got, hold it up and look at it. Do it. Apply it. Obey it. Pray it. Think about it. And look *through* it.

AN INVITATION: SEE

As we receive the Word, we can "read" the world. We can read conversations and circumstances, read novels and movies and people, read current events and politics, read friend and foe. The Scriptures show us how to see, and when we look through them, we see the sacred everywhere in the midst of our ordinary days. We see purpose in pain, we see creative genius in seeming chaos, we see threads of continuity in the shreds of brokenness, we see everywhere the glorious fingerprints of God. We daily glimpse the holy in the ordinary.

When the randomness and heartache and suffering and confusion of this crazy world swirl around us and we're dizzy and disillusioned, the Scriptures serve us like night-vision goggles, enabling us to see God's hidden hand behind all the chaos of life. With practice and patience, we grow in this supernatural ability to see the movement of God in the midst of mundane life. It's incredible! There is nothing more thrilling and life-giving to me than squinting the eyes of my soul and seeing his fingerprints everywhere. Once you start this holy hunt, I'm telling you, you can't quit. You'll be hooked. He is masterful and glorious and truly ingenious and can weave every circumstance for good and glory. When you slip off the drunk goggles and begin seeing your days through the truth of his Word, you'll begin to see him everywhere. Bible reading is no longer a dry spiritual discipline, a box to check; it's embarking on a daily pursuit, the adventure of a lifetime, putting on a supernatural lens that actually lets you see God.

Centuries ago Jean Pierre de Caussade said it like this:

> Those who have abandoned themselves to God lead mysterious lives and receive from him exceptional and miraculous gifts by means of the most ordinary, natural and chance experiences in which there appears to be nothing unusual. The simplest sermon, the most banal conversations, the least erudite books become a source of knowledge and wisdom to these souls by virtue of God's purpose. This is why they carefully pick up the crumbs that clever minds tread under foot, for to them everything is precious and a source of enrichment.[2]

When we see life through the Scriptures, everything is precious and a source of enrichment. But did you notice the condition? "Those who have abandoned themselves to God." The essence of receiving the Word with meekness is receiving the Word with a willingness to obey—that is, receiving the Word having already decided to obey anything God shows you to do. A. W. Tozer wrote, "You can see God anywhere if your mind is set to love and obey Him."[3]

The Scriptures serve us like night-vision goggles, enabling us to see God's hidden hand behind all the chaos of life.

The tricky thing about God is, he doesn't reveal himself for fun. He has no interest in playing hide-and-seek. This isn't a game. Jesus performed all of his miracles for those who truly needed and wanted his healing and delivering touch, but when the Pharisees wanted him to perform some sign, to test him and make him show off like a sideshow in some spiritual circus, Jesus refused. In fact, "He sighed deeply in his spirit and said, 'Why does this generation seek a sign? Truly, I say to you, no sign will be given to this generation.' And he left them, got into the boat again, and went to the other side" (Mark 8:12–13).

The quickest way to quench the Spirit of God in our daily lives is to dishonor his power by wanting him to "do stuff" without wholeheartedly surrendering to his will. Seeing the sacred in the midst of our mundane isn't the end goal; God is. Less of me and more of him is the end goal. His good pleasure and purpose is the end goal. His kingdom come, his will be done, on earth as it is in heaven: this is the end goal.

TODAY

How do we see our ordinary circumstances through the lens of God's Word? What does this process look like in real time? Here's an example from today. We're currently in the middle of a business transaction that has me anxious. Almost a year ago, God put a specific promise on my heart and began confirming it through the Scriptures, through prayer, through recurring dreams, and through the confirmation of trusted, godly people in my life. For about eleven months I've prayed for this thing, waiting sometimes patiently, sometimes impatiently, wondering what it would look like and how it would all come to pass. One week ago, in a flurry of events, it seemed that this promise was coming to pass . . . in a super-awesome way. In fact, it was so much better than I'd dreamed that I went from detached, relaxed, we'll-see-if-it-ever-happens, to oh-my-goodness-this-is-amazing-let's-do-this-can't-move-fast-enough. Four days ago, we had to make a choice regarding the speed at which to pursue this promise.

Now, understand: the promise, to the very best of my understanding, is very clearly from God. I'm not out chasing random dreams. But starting four days ago, after making the legitimate decision to pursue things at our pace, I have had no peace. I am not an anxious person by nature. I tend to be incredibly optimistic (sometimes too much so) and don't worry much. But I felt worried. Here, in front of me, was this amazing promise of God. I could see it. I could taste it. But, there was also a small chance that if we went too slowly (specifically, as slowly as the other party wanted us to go), we'd miss out.

The choice was clear: push forward. Choose our time frame. The other party can deal. Besides, I reasoned, this is a *business* venture. Sure, the other person was clearly upset and overwhelmed and stressed out by our decision, but she wasn't a believer, so of course she was stressed. I said a nice, neat prayer that this poor other person wouldn't feel worried about the whole thing and that she'd learn to trust God.

Then last night I had a fitful dream. In it, I was pushing everyone around me to move forward with this venture, but no one would go fast enough. I was frantic, urging them on, but no one would budge. I woke up early, frustrated and exhausted, anxious about the business transaction, still feeling the agitation of my dream.

Remember how I said sometimes I wake up with the drunk goggles on? Prime example here. The way I saw it, we needed to assert ourselves. We had the upper hand in the deal, so I thought we should handle this business transaction shrewdly to guarantee our success. (Do you sniff out that reference to the shrewd money manager from Luke 16? Like how I used a biblical concept to get my own way? Be on guard against that!) Thankfully, that long-held Bible habit had worn good grooves, and I knew exactly what to do. I pulled back the covers, poured a cup of coffee, opened my Bible, and began to receive the Word. My Old Testament reading was in Leviticus, and it involved a lot of menstruation and leprous skin eruptions, so that didn't seem to apply much to my situation. Then I turned to my New Testament reading in Mark 8. Boom. Surprise, surprise, the day's reading had absolutely nothing to do with shrewd money-managing.

Jesus is predicting his death and resurrection and Peter is appalled. This is not the plan, Jesus! So, Peter takes Jesus aside privately and rebukes him. Ha! Don't you love the incredible honesty of the Scriptures? Peter thinks he's being wise and discreet by correcting Jesus in private, but Jesus turns and gets everyone's attention and rebukes Peter publicly instead, saying, "Get behind me, Satan! For you are not setting your mind on the things of God, but on the things of man" (Mark 8:33).

Whoa. That was it. That was the issue. Like the release of a dam, all the pent-up anxiety came washing out, away, as I realized the truth, as

I saw clearly the situation from God's perspective. Why was I worrying? Because I had set my mind on human things. I was seeing the situation from a worldly perspective and not from God's heavenly perspective. Sure, my situation was different from Peter's, but I was acting just like him, setting my mind on human things. I wrote the verse down in my journal next to the date, then wrote, "What are the 'things of God' in this situation?" I prayed, then continued reading. The very next verses answered my question. Jesus said, "If anyone would come after me, let him deny himself and take up his cross and follow me. For whoever would save his life will lose it, but whoever loses his life for my sake and the gospel's will save it. For what does it profit a man to gain the whole world and forfeit his soul?" (Mark 8:34–36).

There it was. This was what it meant to set my mind on the things of God. Even though this was a business transaction, it was a sacred transaction. There is nothing outside his holy realm. God uses all things to transform our lives from the inside out and display his glory to the world he came to save. Questions began echoing in my mind: "How did you get in this position in the first place? How did you come to this place of even having the ability to consider this transaction? Did it come through your clever schemes and ingenious plans? Did your wealth come from storing up or from lavish, sacrificial giving? Isn't everything you have a wild, extravagant blessing from God in the first place? Why now do you think it depends on your own shrewd business savvy?"

There is nothing outside his holy realm. God uses all things to transform our lives from the inside out.

It was true. Our whole life, which I'll share more about later, has been a journey of letting go, of giving up control. He led us away from our dream home, led us to give half our income away, led us away from our comfy job and security, led us to plant a church among the poor and live on less than we ever thought possible. He led us to give, give, and give some more. And here we were, in a remarkable position to procure the promise of God through his lavish generosity in our lives, and I was jockeying and scheming and demanding my own way. In every single circumstance of life, we'd found God's Word to be true that in losing life we find it; that the way up is down; that the humble are exalted, and the most generous end up with more than they can carry. These truths, these are the "things of God."

And this is life! I'd never before seen the verse from Mark in this way. What does it matter if I "gain the whole world" if I forfeit life? I don't want to merely exist; I want to *live*. Jesus came to give us life to the full! Everyone exists, but only some of us are truly alive. I don't want to lose this precious life of faith, walking in his ways, experiencing his pleasure, seeing his presence constantly in my life. Who cares if I succeed in a thousand business transactions if I lose him?

There was no struggle after this. This wasn't a begrudging "I guess I should call the other party and let them have their way." This was exhilarating! This was the power of God intersecting my ordinary life in a quiet moment, sitting on my bed with an open Bible. This was life! Anxiety was gone. Worry was gone. After conferring with my husband, I immediately acted on the new revelation from God, obeying all the way out of joy, knowing his path is the better path, knowing his ways are always good, knowing my good Father knows best.

And in the obedience, I also saw another beautiful truth: this releasing my desires is for Jesus's sake and the sake of the gospel. Yes, it pleases the heart of God when we obey him no matter what. But you know what else? Our obedience opens up supernatural doors for the gospel to go forth. The reality was, I had been acting no different from an unbeliever in this business transaction. Sure, I offered up an obligatory prayer that the other person "wouldn't worry." But how much greater to choose loss in order that this other person would be blessed. In my situation, this other person just happened to be a single mom who does not know Christ. How much greater to have an opportunity to say, "God wants you to know that he loves you and he is trustworthy. He changed my heart so that you would be blessed. I will gladly give up my rights, because he wants you to know his love for you." This person had seen dozens of Bible verses plastered all over my house, but now she has seen a Bible verse lived out in her life.

The world doesn't pay much attention to our platitudes unless our lives portray the undeniable power of God.

In my experience, the world doesn't pay much attention to our platitudes unless our lives portray the undeniable power of God. They pay attention to people who live upside down. This upside-down kingdom says lose to find, give to gain, die to live. It is a holy invitation to the greatest adventure you'll ever know, seeing the God of the universe work wonders in the midst of the mundane. Come, see.

WAYS TO RECEIVE

Let's finish with some practical ways to receive the Scriptures and see the world through the lens of the Word.

On Our Knees

We've already established that we are to receive the Word with meekness or humility. One way to help humble your heart is to lead with your body. Every morning when I get up, I bow my face to the ground briefly, as a physical reminder to myself that I want to bow my will to his. Often when I am battling my flesh, I run to my room and physically get on my face in prayer. Every time I am done with a speaking engagement, I return somewhere private and get on my knees or face in thanking God. Our physical posture does impact the posture of our hearts. Consider today going lower as a way to humbly receive what he has to say.

In Our Eyes

No shoulds or oughts or finger wagging here, but please understand that no one can receive the Word for you. No matter how many sermons you hear or church services you attend, nothing compares to digging into the Word of God on your own. I've already mentioned my beloved habit of reading through the Bible each year, just three chapters of the Old Testament and one of the New. There are many creative and wonderful Scripture reading plans online and unlimited possible approaches, so ask for God's guidance, determine your course, and do it.

With Our Minds

Just because we're receiving the Word doesn't mean we turn off our minds. We're clearly exhorted in Scripture to love God with all our minds (Luke 10:27). In fact, Jesus said that the planted seed that landed on good soil and bore fruit represented the person who "hears the word and understands it" (Matt. 13:23). Mindless intake without thoughtful reflection, consideration, and even study won't allow the Word to be received and take root in our heart. We must know how to "handle the word of truth," so we can correctly use it to see (see 2 Tim. 2:15). Thankfully, God has given us his Holy Spirit, who will guide us into truth and make known to us the things of God. He's also given us godly guides who can clarify and instruct through commentaries and study Bibles.[4]

On Our Lips

In Deuteronomy 6, God exhorts the children of Israel, "These commandments that I give you today are to be on your hearts. Impress them on your children. Talk about them when you sit at home and when you walk along the road, when you lie down and when you get up" (vv. 6–7 NIV). Just as our children learn through this "on the way" instruction, so do we! The more we talk about the Word, apply it, recite it, and relive it, the more adept we become at looking through the Word to see the world.

Talking in Scripture all day doesn't require you to speak some foreign language. The more conversational and natural you can make it, the better. When reading Scripture, practice saying the verses in an everyday vernacular. Similarly, seek to address the world, circumstances, and sinful behavior in clear biblical terms; that way you're letting God's Word interpret your actions. Pray Scriptures out loud over your family and your life's circumstances. Speak the Word as often as possible. Use your creativity, and let God's Word be ever on your lips.

In Our Ears

Good teachers know that the key to comprehension is using as many different learning styles as possible to teach a particular lesson or skill. While it's critical that we sit quietly in the Word each day, many find it enormously helpful to listen to Scripture as well. With the many technological options we have today, we can listen while we work, drive, exercise. Instead of filling the evening air with a sitcom, consider filling it with God's voice. Different readers, versions, and environments can create memory triggers and increase your capacity to retain Scripture. Songs are also a phenomenal way to receive the Word into our hearts. Music lyrics get stuck in our minds. Consider which ones you'd like stuck there, and play those Scripture-filled songs again and again.

With Each Other

This topic could fill an entire book on its own, but one of the most powerful ways to grow in receiving God's Word is to surround yourself with others who receive it as well. Gathering together as a body of believers is both a scriptural command and a necessary means of spiritual survival. We were never meant to walk alone, and the best way to grow is in a group. No one can receive the Word for us, but the accountability and support of a local church, Bible study, community group, or fellowship can drastically impact the direction of our days. The Bible study at the back of this book is specifically designed for group study, so grab a friend and receive God's Word together.

3

LISTEN: Discern His Voice in Daily Life

Whoever will listen will hear the speaking Heaven.
—A. W. Tozer, *The Pursuit of God*

"You got me, Frank! You got me!"

"Guess what? The bird knocked down a tree! But she put it back up!"

"Don't you understand, Frank? I got you! You understand?"

"Apples, apples, apples! Now she's looking for balloons in the sky."

Crunch, crunch, crunch—spit. Crunch, crunch, crunch—spit.

"I have you, Frank! So there! Oh no! My tank's hit!"

"I guess my birdie's going to have a cupcake!"

Crunch—spit. Crunch, crunch—spit. "Did you hear In-N-Out Burger's coming to Medford?"

"Oh, don't tell me it's *Frank!* You got me!"

This is just a thirty-second excerpt of the soundtrack from a Patterson family road trip. I'm just about to lose my mind at this point. (You may think I already have.) Multiply this by 5,760 and you have a little glimpse of what my life is like, or at least what our annual three-thousand-mile trip to Arizona is like. I am writing this in real time, in the passenger seat. I just took two Ibuprofen. I would love to hear the speaking Heaven right at this moment—I'd love to hear God's voice—but all I can hear is my husband spitting sunflower seeds, the wind-tunnel howl of our car, and the never-ending narratives from the back seat by two children who aren't allowed screen time at home and are therefore overly vocal about their respective iPad games.

Life's noisy. I get it.

I admit I'm less noise tolerant than most. In fact, I'm pretty sure I'm somewhere on the sensory-disorder spectrum. I like my space. I like quiet. TV screens, car radios, crowded spaces, and loud children stress me out. It's God's glorious sense of humor that our life is bursting at the seams with screens and sound. I write online. I homeschool. We lead a boisterous church mostly made up of small children. Eight wonderful souls live within our walls, each with a set of fully functioning vocal chords. I speak at conferences—crowded ones.

I share this with you simply to say that I understand life is loud and that this can pose a real challenge to our mental health. The struggle is real. My kids are still narrating in the back seat, my husband is still spitting seeds (he has an earbud in one ear and is listening to sports radio, which I can hear), and in two hours I'll arrive at a conference where 130 women are waiting. I'm pretty sure they'll all be talking.

How, pray tell, are we to hear God's voice in the midst of this? I would venture to say that many of us don't. This is a tragedy. "Man shall not live on bread alone, but on every word that proceeds out of the mouth of God" (Matt. 4:4 NASB). We live on his words. First and foremost, we hear him through his unchanging written Word, as we saw in the last chapter, but it is his Spirit who takes that truth and communicates it specifically to us in every situation. We need this. We need to hear him speak *to us*. Nothing compares to the glory of hearing him speak to us. This doesn't mean an audible voice per se, but it does mean impressions, things brought to mind, supernatural unction, words resonating with the truth of Scripture that are perfectly applicable to the most specific situation. Hearing the voice of God is the ultimate abundance, the most lavish feast. Conversely, the most tragic kind of famine is not a famine of bread or water but of hearing the words of the Lord (Amos 8:11).

I cannot imagine life without the voice of God speaking hope, guidance, discernment, wisdom, peace, warning, conviction, comfort. Just today I experienced this. We're in the middle of a faith venture, and this morning was one long string of obstacles, discouragements, and seeming roadblocks. I could feel that panicky feeling rising up; I could feel my eyes fill with fearful tears, so I closed them quickly and turned my soul's gaze to him. "Father, I need you," I whispered. Then I listened. In an instant, in the midst of regular life, I heard clearly in my heart: *This is what I have for you. Don't be afraid.*

Hearing the voice of God is the ultimate abundance,
the most lavish feast.

Boom: peace beyond all comprehension. His holy breath gently blows the fear away like dust. The story of Noah suddenly comes to mind, and I'm reminded how hard his own faith journey must have been. Suddenly I identify in a whole new way with his specific obstacles. I'm no longer feeling alone. Peace has filled my heart and mind. I'm ready to turn my attention back to my day—to my kids and home, the bread to bake and the whites to fold. This whole encounter took maybe thirty seconds, but the entire trajectory of my day has turned from feeling hopeless and overwhelmed to a sense of calm, peace, and faith.

We must learn to hear him in the midst. Our restless hearts and anxious minds cannot wait until tomorrow morning's prayer time. We need prayer now. We need to hear him here. See, God knows our lives are noisy, and while he calls us to pull away at times to pray alone, he invites us most often to commune with him in the midst. This is the greatest invitation we'll ever receive.

THE GREATEST INVITATION

When my children were little, we received an invitation to Barn Day. I had heard many people mention that they loved this monthly event, but I knew no details. The only thing I knew was that a family whom I didn't know owned a barn, and they invited homeschool families to come play in it once a month. That sounded fine, but I wasn't necessarily excited to respond. The online invitation didn't give any details, just an address. I took a chance and RSVP'd yes.

The day of, I dressed the kids in mud boots and warm coats (it was a barn, right?) and tried to assure them, rather unconvincingly, that it would be fun. I followed the directions down windy country roads, then turned into a long, paved driveway that wound through the trees. As we came around the final bend, my eyes widened. *That's* the barn?

Before our eyes was the most massive barn-like structure I'd ever seen. To even call it a barn is ridiculous; it was *gorgeous*. Upon walking through the massive eight-foot double doors, we discovered a wonderland: a full-sized gymnasium, upper-level track for walking, a climbing wall with foam-rock pit, an upper-level play structure, ball pit, playhouse, swings, and slides. There were leather couches and a full kitchen, several bathrooms, a special private room for nursing moms, a grand piano, a treadmill, and an entire room filled with athletic equipment, including balls, shoes, nets. You name it, it was there. Enormous windows lined the walls three stories tall, making the whole space light and bright. Kids ran, laughing and playing, while moms sipped lattes and caught up with each other.

I see, I thought. *This is Barn Day.* From that day on, you'd better believe we eagerly responded to the invitation.

I believe that in an infinitely greater way, we don't understand the invitation to prayer. We've heard from a few people that it's something awesome, but we cannot fathom how good the offer is, because our limited experience confines our imagination. As I mentioned earlier, all errant behavior is a result of errant belief. How amazing can a barn really be? Or five minutes of folded hands—how life-changing can that be? Maybe we look to the Lord's Prayer and learn to recite the words, but if we're perfectly honest we find other things far more encouraging. In fact, we find just about everything more energizing than prayer.

But again, we all have a case of the shoulds. So, we tell ourselves that we should pray more because it's such an important spiritual discipline, and we list it once again among our New Year's resolutions and hope this is the year it really sticks. Meanwhile we're making extra Starbucks trips because, let's be honest, we know where our help comes from.

Please hear my heart in this: I do not mean to discount "spiritual disciplines" or New Year's resolutions or any of our attempts at growing with God. But with all due respect, I think this mind-set is our biggest mistake. The problem is, we see prayer as a religious duty instead of an invitation to relationship. So, walk with me for a moment and let's shed those drunk goggles that have us stumbling through life, and look together through the pure, clear lens of God's Word and see the splendor of this glorious invitation to LISTEN to his voice in daily life.

In the beginning, God created his children to walk and talk with him. They would converse naturally, communing in the cool of the day. His children had free and unhindered access to him. They had no need, no lack, no want. But then sin separated. Distrust bred disobedience, and that bite into the forbidden fruit brought tragic consequences: the curse. God's children now knew fear and shame. Their view of God was distorted. Of all that the curse entailed, the most tragic consequence of sin was simply this: God's children hid from him.

The most tragic consequence of sin was simply this: God's children hid from him.

But immediately God launched his redemption plan. Like a master weaver, he began threading lives and promises together, remaining intimately involved in the minutiae of our lives while simultaneously crafting a re-creation plan that captured what was lost in the garden so long ago. But it would take some time. We lost not only our intimacy with God but also our understanding of his greatness, his glory. We would need to relearn who he is. Only as we understand who he is, and who we are, can we begin to taste a bit of that paradise lost.

As we progress through the pages of Scripture we find ourselves in Leviticus, likely a little overwhelmed at the sacrificial system. Here we see God reteaching his people about his holiness. Over and over we see God distinguishing between holy and common, clean and unclean. Only perfect animals were allowed for sacrifice; only the spotless and blameless could atone for the sins of the guilty. The priests had to be ceremonially washed clean before entering God's presence. Only a limited few were given access through the veil, into the Holy of Holies, and these would do so in fear and trembling. Tradition tells us they tied ropes around the ankles of the priests, so that if they were struck dead in the presence of the Lord, the others could drag their bodies out. This seems extreme to us, but God was making a point.

He alone is holy.

This isn't a game, and disobedience is deadly. Sin isn't cute; it separates us from God. The oneness and intimacy we were created for has been lost. Warnings abound: *Don't get too close to the presence of God.* If you touch the mountain of God, you'll die. If you look upon the face of God, you'll die. If you come into his presence in a flippant way, you'll die. This God parts seas, rains down bread from heaven, and brings water flowing from a rock. He can pour out plagues, throw down kings, rout armies, and annihilate entire nations in one fell swoop. Nothing is too difficult for him. The nation of Israel knew their God and knew their place. They lived in holy fear, outside the veil.

Until God tore it in two from top to bottom.

In an unexpected plot twist, God's only Son is born in a barn. In the most appalling manner imaginable, he slips on skin and surprises the whole world by eagerly embracing the unclean. He eats with drunkards and prostitutes, touches lepers and corpses. He shuns the should-ers and aggravates the law abiders while welcoming women, children, and tax collectors, the despised and devalued of the day. The world is caught unawares: This is what God is like? He is holy and mighty *and* humble and kind? Here, all the authority, power, and glory of the Father are fully revealed in his Son, Jesus Christ. Suddenly God is accessible once again. All who brush the hem of his garment are healed. Oh glorious day! *We can touch God.*

But then, God goes even further.

In the span of one week's time, Jesus goes from hero to criminal. Just days after the crowds are calling, "Hosanna!" they're screaming, "Crucify him!" Even after receiving sight, they're blinded again. So, Jesus, the pure and perfect Lamb of God, takes away the sin of the world by dying on a cross and receiving in himself the righteous wrath of a just and holy God. All the punishment we deserve, borne away in Jesus's body. And at the exact moment when Jesus declares, "It is finished," and breathes his last, the veil of the temple is torn in two from top to bottom (Mark 15:38; see also Lev. 21:23).

Limitless access freely granted. This is good news beyond our comprehension!

Now, because of Jesus, we have access to God. No longer do we go through a priest—we are priests (1 Peter 2:9). No longer must we only offer prayers in a temple—our bodies are his temple (1 Cor. 6:19). Our lives are an altar. The world is God's sanctuary. We live in the Holy of Holies. Everywhere we go we can immediately access the presence of God. The same God who poured out plagues, routed armies, annihilated nations, and rained down bread from heaven, this same God has opened the door and called us back into his presence.

We live in the Holy of Holies. Everywhere we go we can immediately access the presence of God.

But then, this same God goes even further.

He puts his Spirit in us, making his presence closer than our skin, and invites us to a thriving intimate relationship with him, closer than any earthly relationship, one where we can openly and freely relate with him, like a child with her dad.

The King of Kings. The God of the universe. The Creator of heaven and earth. The Eternal One. The Almighty God . . .

. . . is our Dad.

And he invites us onto his lap for a quiet conversation. He welcomes all our questions, even the ones we think we shouldn't ask. He listens with eternal patience. And then, wonder of all wonders, he makes us mind-boggling promises within the context of this Father-child relationship. The same God who can rout armies, annihilate nations, still storms, and raise the dead, he leans in close to us in the person of Jesus and says,

> "Whatever you ask in prayer, you will receive, if you have faith." (Matt. 21:22)

> "Whatever you ask in prayer, believe that you have received it, and it will be yours." (Mark 11:24)

> "Whatever you ask in my name, this I will do, that the Father may be glorified in the Son. If you ask me anything in my name, I will do it." (John 14:13–14)

> "Truly, truly, I say to you, whatever you ask of the Father in my name, he will give it to you. Until now you have asked nothing in my name. Ask, and you will receive, that your joy may be full." (John 16:23–24)

> "Ask, and it will be given to you. . . . If you then, who are evil, know how to give good gifts to your children, how much more will your Father who is in heaven give good things to those who ask him!" (Matt. 7:7, 11)

Are you beginning to grasp the glory of God's invitation? Its extravagance is overwhelming. It's ridiculous grace. Our minds cannot begin to comprehend the greatness of the offer to commune with almighty God.

That is why I spent most of my Christian life trying to explain away these verses. They seemed too good. Too extravagant. Too—dare I say it?—dangerous. Didn't God know how greedy I could be? Surely giving us sinners a carte blanche promise that he would do "whatever" is not a good idea. Couldn't he see all the prosperity gospel stuff that would surface as a result? If I were God, I would never have given such lavish promises. We humans are way too wicked for such generosity. Right? So, whenever I saw people starting to drift into these dangerous waters, especially when I saw them praying for shallow things like healing from sickness or a better salary, I was quick to remind them that we should only ask for really spiritual stuff like patience and salvation for unsaved uncles.

I'm exaggerating, but there's a bit of truth to this. It wasn't until I understood God's extravagant promises in the context of relationship, and quit divorcing "spiritual" things from my ordinary life, that I began to taste and see the glory and adventure of interacting with God in prayer. It begins by returning to relationship with our heavenly Dad.

OUR FATHER

My daughter, Heidi, is seven and shy. I was the same. I was so painfully shy as a child that at church I would hide under my mom's skirt, desperate to avoid the attention of some new, overly friendly stranger. When we're out in public, my daughter is the same. One-word, barely audible answers are all that most people get. We have family members who have yet to ever receive a hug from her. She's lavish in her love; it just takes time for her to open up.

But you better believe that when we're at home, she's a chatterbox. She's my mini-me, constantly at my side, wanting to help knead bread dough or fold clothes or scrub the toilet (really!). She loves to be near me, supplying a steady stream of conversation throughout the day. (She's sitting on the arm of my chair as I type these words.) At night, when we're snuggled down under her quilt, she shares any "yucky thoughts" she had that day. These are scary things, or sad things, or things that made her anxious. She's quite sensitive, so there are usually plenty of these yucky thoughts, but she openly shares them with me every night before bed.

I never have to coerce my daughter to talk to me. I never have to tell her to work on the "discipline" of conversing with me. We're in relationship. We talk. She's constantly pouring out her heart and asking me questions. Sure, she does most of the talking, but I say stuff too. And she listens.

The other day I was reflecting on this, and I remarked to Jeff, "Can you imagine if we got a stranger off the street, brought him into Heidi's room, and commanded her to tell him all her 'yucky thoughts,' all her innermost fears and anxieties? If we told her she needed to grow in this 'discipline'? Can you imagine?"

The analogy may seem absurd, but there's some similarity in how some of us approach growing in prayer. Heidi naturally pours out her heart to me each day because of our relationship. Not because she wants to grow in a spiritual discipline. Because I'm her mom. She's my daughter. She loves me; I love her. That's enough.

Any attempt to grow spiritually without growing relationally will only lead to religious slavery.

My own prayer life wasn't transformed, nor does it continue to be transformed, through a New Year's resolution or a renewed commitment to "spiritual disciplines." It isn't that spiritual disciplines are of no value; discipline is critical for Christ followers. We are, after all, *disciples*. But our discipline always flows from a relationship, so when we seek "the spiritual disciplines" apart from relationship, we're bound for failure and frustration. The disciples weren't told to follow a movement, a religion, or a philosophy; they were called to follow a person. Jesus simply said, "Follow me." Any attempt to grow spiritually without growing relationally will only lead to religious slavery. We need to read that again: any attempt to grow spiritually without growing relationally will only lead to religious slavery.

We're constantly in danger of drifting away from sonship toward slavery. See, Christianity is simply the story of the Father sending his perfect Son to bring home his lost children. The gospel is the welcome home. No longer slaves, but sons. No longer orphans, but heirs. We read this throughout the New Testament:

> When the fullness of time had come, God sent forth his Son, born of woman, born under the law, to redeem those who were under the law, so that we might receive adoption as sons. And because you are sons, God has sent the Spirit of his Son into our hearts, crying, "Abba! Father!" So you are no longer a slave, but a son, and if a son, then an heir through God. (Gal. 4:4–7)

> All who are led by the Spirit of God are sons of God. For you did not receive the spirit of slavery to fall back into fear, but you have received the Spirit of adoption as sons, by whom we cry, "Abba! Father!" The Spirit himself bears witness with our spirit that we are children of God, and if children, then heirs—heirs of God and fellow heirs with Christ, provided we suffer with him in order that we may also be glorified with him. (Rom. 8:14–17)

> See what kind of love the Father has given to us, that we should be called children of God. (1 John 3:1)

Nowhere in the New Testament does God refer to us as slaves. He calls us his children, and in joyful response we call ourselves his eager, voluntary servants, because he has so lavishly loved us that we want to offer ourselves to him freely in return. But this happy servant's heart always flows out of knowing our identity first and foremost as his kids.[1]

Every time Jesus teaches on prayer, he emphasizes this Father-child relationship we have with God. We cannot miss this. He specifically tells us to pray, "Our Father," keeping this intimate relationship at the forefront of our minds and hearts (Matt. 6:9). This is why our attempts to grow in spiritual discipline apart from relationship lead only to religious rigmarole. Jesus made this clear when he taught against the hypocrites who loved to "pray" publicly in order to be seen as spiritual, and against the Gentiles who "heaped up empty phrases" in order to get their way with God. Jesus says instead, "When you pray, go into your room and shut the door and pray to your Father who is in secret. And your Father who sees in secret will reward you. . . . Your Father knows what you need before you ask him" (Matt. 6:6–8).

See, the Gentiles and hypocrites were engaging in religious activity, not genuinely communing with God. The hypocrites were doing it in such a way that those around them would be impressed. The Gentiles were doing it in such a way that God would be impressed. Both were a show. Neither of them understood the heart of the Father. Jesus says, "Just pray simply and honestly to your Father. He knows what you need already, so it's not that you need to 'fill him in' on what's going on. He just wants you to come be with him, share your needs and heart with him, hear from him, partner with him, be with him."

A transformed prayer life begins with this understanding: God is my Father; I am his child. In order to discern his voice, we have to determine who he is. This isn't merely a mystical experience with some impersonal force. It is the intimate conversation between a Father and his child. Our goal is to discern our Daddy's voice in daily life.

WHAT A CHILD IS LIKE

As I type these words, my daughter is snuggled up next to me with her head resting on my stomach. She's been mostly quiet, but over the past few minutes she's softly spoken a thought: "I loved seeing the ducks today." A question: "When am I going to Madison's house?" And a praise: "I love you, Mommy. You're the best mommy in the world." In just minutes she has shared her heart, sought clarity about the future, and expressed authentic praise. Sounds like a pretty solid understanding of prayer to me. No wonder Jesus told us we must change to become childlike (Matt. 18:3). He wasn't just being cute. He was giving us an important spiritual secret!

So, what is a child like? I have several of them surrounding me as I type this, so it's fairly easy to make observations. Three key characteristics come to mind that would enrich our communion with God.

First, children are completely self-absorbed. When my son bursts into my bedroom each morning, he's already in mid sentence, all his thoughts about dinosaurs and the Ice Age and Beethoven's Fifth Symphony spilling out into space. He doesn't stop and think, "Wait, I can only talk to her about adult things, not these silly things on my mind." Of course not. I want to hear what's on his mind. Those things will probably change as he matures, but the only way to build a relationship is to begin where we are now.

The future-you cannot approach God. Only the you who you are today can.

To genuinely pray, to connect with the heart of our Father, we must simply begin where we are now. The biggest obstacle to intimacy is waiting until we feel prayerful or spiritual, or trying to get our thoughts all neat and tidy before we begin. In Paul Miller's life-giving and supremely practical book, *A Praying Life*, he explains, "If you don't begin with where you are, then where you are will sneak in the back door. Your mind will wander to where you are weary."[2]

Isn't this true? If your mind wanders to your son's struggles in school, start there! If your mind drifts to financial anxieties, start there! There is really no sense in trying to pretend with God. He already knows all our thoughts, so any attempts to mask our fears or selfishness are silly, and sort of offensive, if you think about it. Who are we to think we can fool him? Jesus calls this hypocrisy. Instead, let's come to him like a child approaches her loving father.

Second, children tend to express all their thoughts out loud. Anyone with children is familiar with the common scenario of having a small (or not-so-small) child blurt out some embarrassing comment in public: "Why does that lady have such a big tummy?" "Mommy, my bottom itches!" As we mature, we learn to keep these thoughts to ourselves, but praying out loud definitely helps us cultivate a childlike attitude in prayer in several ways.

For one, praying aloud encourages us to freely express our innermost selves to God, which cultivates intimacy. While we're wise to filter our words for people, the one place we're encouraged to "pour out our hearts" is with God. It's foolish to vent our feelings to others, but it's godly to vent them to God. He's the only one who is never tainted by our mixed bag of emotions. It's not gossip when you're talking to God! We're wise to go to the throne before we go to the phone.

Praying out loud also keeps our minds from wandering (as much). Let's face it: we're praying one minute and making a mental grocery list the next. We're hopelessly distractible. It's much easier to focus when there are audible words coming out of our mouths. It also helps give perspective to what we're praying. Some things seem one way in our minds, but when they're spoken into the air, we can see them more clearly. This is especially true concerning confession. It's easy to think a confessional thought about something we've done; it's quite another thing to say it out loud.

Third, children are frank about their faults. That is, kids call spades, spades; they haven't learned the deceptive art of dressing up difficult situations with sophisticated words. A critical component of childlike prayer is confession, and the English word *confess* is a translation of the Greek word *homologeo*, which literally means, "To say the same." That is, we agree to say the same about something that God says about it. In other words, I'll call it what he calls it.

This is powerful in prayer! So often in our adult sophistication we become brilliant wordsmiths and create clever names for our sin. We love to rename it in order to make it sound better. For example: an affair. An affair is a special event I attend with my spouse. The correct word for having sex with someone else's spouse is *adultery*.

God our Father has names for things. He is clear. When I say, "I'm just struggling with feeling like no one appreciates all the hard work I do. I really deserve some recognition," that is called pride. When I say, "I'm just struggling because she has this big beautiful house and we're just barely making ends meet," that is called envy.

Why is this critical? Because until we name it, we can't ditch it! We can't repent of a "struggle." We can only repent of *sin*. As long as we dress it up in flowery language, we'll never flee from it. God doesn't command us to call sin, sin because he wants to rub our faces in it. He has no interest in humiliating us; he wants to free us. He knows that as long as we call it something lovely like an "affair," we won't understand the seriousness of sin—that it takes us far, far away from him. Remember, this isn't a game. Sin isn't cute. I don't want to cuddle up with what Christ died to free me from. Sin only leads to death. It only leads to destruction, bondage, grief. He wants me, his child, to be free.

———— ⚘ ————

We can't repent of a "struggle."
We can only repent of *sin*.

So, we deal frankly, confess openly, speak honestly, refuse to go through religious motions or hide our true selves. We come just as we are, runny-nosed, self-absorbed children in need of the Father's love and care. Then, once we embody what children are like, we'll be ready to learn what God's children do.

CHILDREN ASK

Most of Jesus's teaching on prayer revolved around the all-important component of a parent-child relationship, *asking*. Over and over, Jesus tells us to ask.

Kids ask a lot of questions. They ask for stuff. They ask for snacks. They ask where babies come from and why airplanes don't fall from the sky. They're constantly seeking answers. They aren't overly concerned with how appropriate their questions are or how preposterous their requests—they just keep on asking, knowing that their trusted parent will sift through all that.

Specifically, children tend to ask with persistence and faith. There is nothing too outlandish for a child to request, and they have no problem asking the same thing three dozen times in a row. Though it can try our patience as parents, I have often prayed for this same persistence and faith in my own prayer life.

However, child*like* does not mean child*ish*. We want to continue in the first, not the second. When I taught my toddler son about making requests in prayer, the very first thing he asked God for was pizza. Ha! I inwardly doubted, but you better believe my jaw dropped when my husband came home from work that very night with a piece of leftover pizza he'd had from a meeting. I could barely believe my eyes, but my son happily devoured that slice and thanked God for answering his prayer! That is precious and appropriate for a two-year-old, but thankfully my son now prays for healing, salvation, and encouragement for others (and still, occasionally, pizza). Though he's still a child, I see that he's developing a strong understanding of what to ask God for in prayer. This is key. James says we have not because we ask not, but then says we have not when we ask because we ask amiss (James 4:2–3). Clearly, we must move beyond our childish demands and desires. But how do we know what to ask for?

Interestingly, the disciples' first request was simply this: "Lord, teach us to pray." That's a great first request! I suggest we never stop making this simple request. We know this is the will of the Father, so we can always ask with confidence, knowing we have what we ask.

That first request will then guide all the rest. As Jesus teaches us to pray, we will have a greater and greater understanding of what to ask for because we'll have an increasing understanding of who God is and where he's headed. All of our requests flow out of our understanding of our Father—his nature, his ways, his purposes. I'm convinced we don't need a sophisticated understanding of every situation as much as we need a childlike knowledge of who God is. But how do we gain this insight into the heart of God? How can we align our heart's desires with his? We do another thing that children do: we listen.

CHILDREN LISTEN

It was the child Samuel, early as a priest-in-training, who spoke the oft-quoted, beautiful words, "Speak, Lord, for your servant hears" (see

1 Sam. 3:9–10). From an early age he tuned his ear to God. This childlike attitude enabled him to maintain a lifelong listening relationship with the one true God. While all the other bigwig prophets and priests were listening to themselves, Samuel was listening to God. So, too, only as we listen are we able to pray according to God's will. Only as we listen will we hear his insight, wisdom, and discernment.

While all the other bigwig prophets and priests were listening to themselves, Samuel was listening to God.

Discernment is the difference between living childlike and living childishly. Discernment is the mark of maturity (Heb. 5:12–14). Paul wrote, "It is my prayer that your love may abound more and more, with knowledge and all discernment" (Phil. 1:9). Discernment is essential if we are to *let* our days transform our lives, and especially essential as we listen with spiritual ears. Not all that's whispered in our ears is from God. We must distinguish between the various voices. The world, our flesh, and the enemy are all very loud, but as we ask God to speak, we then intentionally turn down the world's noise, quiet our flesh, resist the devil, and tune in to the still, small voice of God. Then we grow in our ability to perceive the will of God (Rom. 12:1–2).

How, exactly? One of the best ways to grow in effective prayer is to study the various prayers in the Scriptures. These will powerfully shape our own. For example, the apostle Paul's opening prayer for the Colossians reads, "And so, from the day we heard, we have not ceased to pray for you, asking that you may be filled with the knowledge of his will in all spiritual wisdom and understanding, so as to walk in a manner worthy of the Lord, fully pleasing to him: bearing fruit in every good work and increasing in the knowledge of God; being strengthened with all power, according to his glorious might, for all endurance and patience with joy" (Col. 1:9–11). Notice Paul prays that they be filled with the knowledge of God's will (discernment), walk in a manner that fully pleases him (our sole vocation), bear fruit (please him), increase in the knowledge of God (knowing his heart), and be strengthened with power for endurance (*hupomone*).

Paul's prayer is essentially a twofold request that teaches us a tremendous amount about the nature of true prayer: (1) knowing God and his will, and (2) obtaining power to perform his will.

First, we pray to know God's heart, what he wants. Then we pray for the power to carry out his desire. This is why prayer goes hand in hand with Scripture. If we really want to know God, to know his heart and what he's like, we will search his Word, hold it up and look at everything through it, and learn to actually see as he sees in order to act as he would act. We can do what Jesus did.

This prayer unleashes the power of God to do on earth as he does in heaven. In heaven there is no sickness, no starvation, no sin, no strife. God wants his kingdom to come through our prayers.

Now, to do this we need power. Specifically, we need power for endurance and patience with joy (Col. 1:11). Did you catch that? Endurance. You know that word, right? You guessed it: *hupomone*. Yet again *hupomone* is what we need, and it is through prayer that God grants to us this *hupomone*.

Notice that Paul prays also for patience. So, what's the difference between *hupomone* and patience? We already determined that *hupomone* "is the spirit which no circumstance in life can ever defeat and which no event can ever vanquish. It is the ability to deal triumphantly with anything that life can do to us."[3] Yes!

Patience, on the other hand, is the Greek word *makrothumia*, which is patience with people. "It is the quality of mind and heart which enables a man so to bear with people that their unpleasantness and maliciousness and cruelty will never drive him to bitterness, that their folly will never drive him to irritation, that their unloveliness will never alter his love. It is the spirit which never loses patience with, belief in, and hope for people."[4]

Yeah, so, we're gonna need a hefty dose of that too. Order me up some Spirit-given *hupomone* and *makrothumia*.

Paul is praying that no circumstances can defeat the Colossians' strength and no human being can defeat their love. And what, according to verse 11, is the accompanying fruit of this kind of endurance and patience? Joy. True joy is the fruit of such endurance and patience—a radiance that not all the sorrows of life can overshadow.

Paul is praying that no circumstances can defeat the Colossians' strength and no human being can defeat their love.

So, the heart of prayer is, *God, I want you. Show me yourself and help me listen and discern your will, then give me the power to perform that will. Give me victorious endurance over every circumstance and loving patience with every person. And through all this, give me your abundant joy, which no circumstance or person can ever take from me.*

Amen.

HINDRANCES TO HEARING

Let's return to my family's road trip. It didn't take long before our kids were tired of my typing and Jeff's sports radio listening. They wanted us to listen to them, so Heidi made this simple request: "Please take out those plug things because they make you not hear me."

Fair enough. And so, I believe the heart of God might echo Heidi's as well: he may wish for us to take out those "plug things," whatever they may be, so we can hear his voice a bit more clearly. As we close this chapter, let's look briefly at three "plug things" that are hindrances to hearing God.

Earplugs ➻ *Pride*

Nothing hinders our receptiveness to the voice of God more than pride, and nothing encourages a sensitivity to his Spirit more than humility. God opposes the proud but gives grace to the humble. Humility unstops our ears and lets us hear the voice of our humble King. We will find that we hear him with increasing clarity the more we embrace our humble identity as a child and surrender fully to the will of our loving Father.

Deafness ⤳ Sin

Sadly, when we ignore sin in our lives, we lose our sensitivity to God's voice. Eventually our spiritual eardrums become calloused and less able to discern his voice in our daily lives. Obedience keeps our hearing keen. Ignoring God's voice dulls our ability to discern. So the first thing to daily ask God is, "Search me and know me. . . . See if there is any wicked way in me, and lead me in the way everlasting" (Ps. 139:23–24, my rendering). Then when he reveals sin to us, we confess it—that is, we say the same thing about it that he says—and enjoy this glorious promise: "If we confess our sins, he is faithful and just to forgive us our sins and to cleanse us from all unrighteousness" (1 John 1:9).

Noise ⤳ Competing Voices

We already determined that life is noisy. As if the conflicting outer voices aren't enough, there are conflicting inner voices too. We're a complex tangle of thoughts, feelings, and desires. We must learn to be still and know that he is God. Only as we offer our lives as living sacrifices can we choose daily not to be conformed to this world but be transformed by the renewing of our minds (Rom. 12:1–2). We are told, "Above all else, guard your heart, for everything you do flows from it" (Prov. 4:23 niv). We guard our hearts by guarding our minds by guarding what we hear (Phil. 4:7–8). We are wise to protect our precious souls from the toxic noise of the world.

As the great prophet Elijah discovered, God isn't often found in the wind and the fire, the flashiest signs and the loudest shouts. He is found in the still, small voice. He whispers to us in our daily lives when we quiet down enough to hear. Then we, as his children, draw near, share our hearts, ask our questions, confess our sin, express our praise, listen, and discern his voice in daily life.

4

ENGAGE: Enter In

When Christ is Lord, nothing is secular.
—John Stott

WE ARE READY TO enter into "real" life. We've learned to first *look* to what is physically invisible and *listen* to what is physically inaudible. We've placed the unseen, unheard *real* spiritual world above what physically assaults our senses each day. We've ditched the drunk goggles, put on the clear lens of God's perfect Word, and begun to discern his gentle voice. We've *let* him in. We're ready to face the day.

As I type these words I am just finishing my quiet time. In a matter of moments my kids will stir, our housemates will rise, the day will begin. It's Sunday morning, my pastor husband is already on his way, and soon we'll be breakfasting and bed-making and dressing and combing and covering all our bases as we head to our worship gathering. The *looking* and the *listening* still continue, but it's time to engage in life.

Now, when you read that I am married to a pastor, perhaps you think my life has a little extra holy sparkle to it. Perhaps you suspect the sacred is in my mundane a little more than it is in yours. Your husband might be a plumber; you might be a bus driver. You might be a single mom heroically juggling two jobs—or a stay-at-home mom with a gaggle of kids. So, just to be clear: my mundane is no more sacred than yours. When Christ is Lord, nothing is secular. In fact, a string of dead-end jobs was where my husband and I truly discovered the sacred mundane. If you'll indulge me for a moment, I'd love to back up and share our stumbling, fumbling, falling-backward journey into a life of wholeness, where sacred/secular divisions do not exist.

"PAD TREE"

"Pad tree" was where I began to embrace the sacred mundane. It was just days after everything fell apart. Jeff and I had been working full-time at a church, teaching at a ministry training school, leading foreign mission trips, and helping oversee a large, thriving college ministry. I was writing and codirecting gospel dramas performed to thousands, and dozens of people had come to faith in Christ through them. We had just purchased a new little home and celebrated our first anniversary. Everything seemed perfect. Then.

Full of optimism, we jumped at what seemed a fabulous ministry opportunity in sunny California. It appeared to be a dream come true. We fasted and prayed, seeking God's guidance whether to go, and though we received mixed messages from trusted advisors, we took a step of faith (naiveté?) and jumped at the opportunity. Over the course of several months, we carefully cut ties with life up north. We visited each of our supporters, thanking them and explaining that we'd no longer need financial support, as we would be provided a salary. We rented out our home and made long, tearful good-byes to our families and friends. It felt like leaving our entire lives behind, but we were hopeful that this new opportunity would be better than we could ever imagine. Like Naaman loading up his chariot with lofty expectations, we drove our loaded U-Haul down the interstate, full of anticipation for this ministry venture.

Now, I've decided to delete the details of what happened because the people involved are brothers and sisters in Christ, and love keeps no record of wrongs. Though we felt misled and hurt, Jeff and I would never want someone to recount our failures (of which there are plenty!) publicly and permanently, on paper. Forgiveness frees us to select the details of all debts and push *delete*. Jesus paid it all. It is finished.

Suffice it to say, things didn't go as planned and it was painful. When everything went down, with tears streaming down my cheeks, I looked Jeff in the eye and told him my three-word plan: "Take me home."

Forgiveness frees us to select the details of all debts and push delete. Jesus paid it all. It is finished.

In that moment, Jeff took my hands in his, and in his gentle way, urged me to trust. "If you want, I will take you home. But let's pray. Let's sleep on it. God may be in this. Let's enter into *here*."

I squinted my eyes at him. Enter into this? This disaster? Why on earth would I want to enter into this? We had no money, no job, nothing. Our new "home" was a filthy, windowless office space with rotted floors, molded food, and piles of old belongings left behind by someone else. Absolutely nothing was as I thought it would be. Everything inside me wanted to escape. Run back home. Back to comfort. Back to friends. Back to "ministry" and the sacred life that fit really well in my paradigm of what following God was supposed to be like. But, I reasoned in that moment, maybe Jeff was right. Maybe God wanted us to enter into here.

The following Monday morning I had a job. I'd slipped on my only pair of heels and marched into Nordstrom Rack, where a friend of mine was working. The women's department manager looked at my résumé for ten seconds and told me I would start the following Monday. The first day I arrived at work, no one knew I was coming. After waiting thirty minutes for my boss, I finally caught a woman's eye.

"Hi, I'm looking for Lynn, the women's manager." She looked at me in incomprehension. "*Lynn*. I'm looking for Lynn. Today is my first day of work."

"Ah. Okay. You come me." Her English was broken, but she held up a hand to show I'd said enough and summoned me to follow her. I wordlessly followed her out into the main part of the store.

Finally, I asked, "So, what is your name?"

"Kobra." Cobra? Like the venomous snake?

"Oh. Well it's nice to meet you, Cobra. Thank you for training me." She nodded deeply in acknowledgment, and we walked in silence to the middle of the store. She motioned with her hand to a large general vicinity.

"You pad tree." Now I stared at her in incomprehension. I'm pad tree? Was that like pad Thai? Did we all have code names in this line of work?

"All dis"—she motioned to the mountainous heaps of crumpled clothes piled on each round clothing rack—"you clean." She gesticulated wildly to show that it should all be gone. Then she went to a rack and fingered the hung clothes. "Sort." She looked at me. I nodded. "Size." I nodded again. She walked to an X-shaped rack for displaying clothing. "Color." She put a purple sweater next to another purple sweater, and I nodded again. She placed her palms together and nodded deeply, like a bow, then turned and shuffled away as she'd done before, pulling her cart behind her, staring at the floor. I took a deep breath and began, piece by crumpled piece, to pull each article of clothing off the top to rehang them.

Eventually it dawned on me that I was responsible for *pad three*, the petite and plus-sized portion of the store. At one point a woman asked me if we carried Tommy Bahama. I stared at her, blink-blink, and then fled to find Kobra to ask who Tommy Bahama was and if we carried him. I eventually met my boss, who seemed thoroughly amused that I'd graduated summa cum laude yet hadn't a trace of retail comprehension and couldn't figure out how to use the intercom. I just tried to smile a lot and told her thank you whenever she gave me a job to do, then thanked her again at the end of each day as I clocked out. She laughed at me. "I have no idea why you thank me all the time, but I sure love having you here."

When exactly it happened I don't remember, but at some point, amidst the clothes racks, while sliding on sleeves and sorting by size, the realization became clear: the sacred mundane story God had begun years ago was still being written in my life. This was redemptive work. God really was here. Every space is sacred when we *let* him in and choose to truly enter in ourselves.

BARIUM RESIN VIALS

We thought nothing could rival the bleakness of our living space, but Jeff's new sacred work trumped all. With a civil engineering degree, he applied for forty-seven construction management positions. No reply. Finally, he was offered a temp job at a place called BioTech—doing what, he wasn't exactly sure.

On his first day he was directed to a dimly lit back room filled with tiny workstations and men in lab coats and goggles. He was given a lab coat a size too small, with the name Vladimir embroidered across the front. The sleeves reached about three quarters of the way down his arms. He was instructed to keep his goggles on at all times. *Never remove your goggles.*

He sat down at his workstation next to Aneel, a Middle Eastern man with a long gray beard. He looked about seventy-five. He was partially lame in both legs, so he shuffled along with a cane. Jeff introduced himself cheerfully and held out his hand. Aneel shook his hand respectfully, looked Jeff in the eye, and said with grave seriousness, "Get out of here as soon as you can."

Jeff's job was to fill miniature vials with 1.0000 ounce of barium resin, using a six-way pipette. This specially engineered pipette had to be balanced and handled with extreme care to ensure the proper dispensing, which meant hand cramps were an everyday occurrence. Jeff's quota? He was told that his daily goal should be twenty-five thousand vials. Confident in his competency, he set to work with fervor, only to look up at four o'clock and realize he'd only done five thousand. Aneel once again warned him, "Never, never do twenty-five thousand. If you do, they will make you do more. They are mean, mean men. Never do twenty-five thousand." Jeff assured him he didn't think that would ever be a problem.

It was here, among the barium vials, that Jeff's sacred mundane moment came. One day, Aneel was home sick. Without his normal conversant, Jeff decided to use earbuds and listen to a sermon from 1 Samuel 18. In it the pastor examined why God gave David thirteen years of trials and wandering, confusion and grief, living in caves and running for his life, before God placed him as king. The pastor explained that all of this was God's holy preparation of David's heart.

In other words, all of life is a sacred seminary for our souls.

All of life is a sacred seminary for our souls.

If our life aim is to know and please God, bearing fruit in every good work, we are automatically enrolled in the life curriculum of the Master Teacher. Sure, we can choose to audit. We can show up when we want to but skip the difficult parts. Or we can enter in. We can engage with life fully, not escaping when the pressure builds or painful moments come, but rather, diving into the divine every single day.

As Jeff sat, hunched over his hundreds of vials, God's voice enveloped his heart. All of life was preparation because all of life was sacred. There were many things around us that made us grieved, sad, and frustrated, but it was all part of God's preparation for the sacred work he'd called us to. In fact, this *was* the sacred work. How would we respond? Would we escape or would we engage and choose to see him there in it all?

We knew how to see him in the conventional, churchy ways, in powerful prayer meetings and exhilarating worship services, but what about seeing him holding a six-fingered barium pipette? Was he in the midst of messy clothing racks and blistered, aching feet? My job wasn't feeding orphans, digging wells, or preaching sermons but selling Cole Haan and Juicy Couture, arguably cultivating the consumerist culture I already despised. How could this be sacred?

It could only be sacred if Jesus was Lord of it. Lord of me. A. W. Tozer wrote, "Let a man sanctify the Lord God in his heart and he can thereafter do no common act."[1] When Christ is Lord of my life, everything I do is sacred. I fully enter in by letting him be Lord and Master of it all, then by receiving the gift of now, the gift of here, whatever and wherever that is.

All of life, under the command of Christ, is sacred. The kingdom of God is wherever Christ is king. "There is not a square inch in the whole domain of our human existence over which Christ, who is Sovereign over all, does not cry: 'Mine!'"[2] This earth is his. I am his. No matter what our job, status, situation, or position, all of life is sacred work when carried out by image bearers containing the Holy Spirit of God.

Though the scenery changed, for fifty months Jeff and I staggered and stumbled through this life-seminary season of confusion, feeling forgotten, shelved by God. It wasn't always pretty. Jeff laid sewer pipe. We lived with my parents. We constantly battled doubt and discouragement, but God forged faith in us through the heat and the hammering of this struggle. He forced us out of "church work" to prove that his presence was everywhere if we would humble ourselves enough to seek and serve him there. God even birthed my blog during a particularly dark season of discouragement when I felt most alone and confused. Writing forced me to focus my spiritual eyes and detect his presence, even in the darkness. Though I don't want to do it again, this difficult season was where we ditched the sacred/secular duality and learned to live the sacred mundane, where we learned to fully engage and enter in.

THE SACRED/SECULAR DUALITY

Let's consider the theology behind all this. We already determined that all of life is a sacred sacrifice of praise, that the presence of God transforms ordinary into holy. So far so good, right? What blindsides us along the way is this old sacred/secular duality. A. W. Tozer writes, "One of the greatest hindrances to internal peace which the Christian encounters is the common habit of dividing our lives into two areas—the sacred and the secular."[3] Though few of us would say we see life this way, we tend to make these dangerous divisions on a daily basis.

For example, we label books and music "Christian" or "non-Christian." We send our children either to "Christian" school or "public" school. We refer to our "secular" jobs and our "ministry" jobs. Throughout our week we engage in the supposedly sacred acts of prayer, Bible study, church attendance, and so forth. But then we inevitably inhabit the supposedly secular world where we work, eat, sleep, clean, dress, wash, brush our teeth, fold laundry, go to the doctor, and wipe counters, noses, and bottoms. The reality is that the second list is much longer than the first, and this leaves us frustrated. We wish we could do more "for God," or be more involved in church affairs, or give attention to our "spiritual life," but the reality of work and daily duties leaves little time for holier pursuits. How do we follow Jesus *here*?

Now, it is understandable that we feel the disconnect. We do inhabit two worlds. Every day we engage in a physical world and a spiritual world. We have regenerate spirits—awake and alive to God—and yet live in bodies still susceptible to sin, weakness, and disease. Who can blame us if we fall into this pit of division? After all, don't we have two natures?

No, we don't. We who have been born again have been made alive in Christ and no longer must obey the lusts of the flesh. We don't have two natures. Scripture makes it clear—those of us who "were by nature children of wrath" have been "made . . . alive together with Christ" (Eph. 2:3–5). We do not just add a new spirit to our old, corrupt one; we are a whole new creation, made alive where we were dead. Second Corinthians 5:17 explains: "Therefore, if anyone is in Christ, he is a new creation. The old has passed away; behold, the new has come."

Everyone, saved or not, lives a whole life. A person who has not placed her faith in Christ is by nature a child of wrath (Eph. 2:3). She too is whole—wholly dead in sin (v. 1). She is utterly incapable of pleasing God or living a sacred life (Rom. 8:8). But we who are bought by the blood of Christ, ransomed and regenerate and given life anew, are whole as well—wholly his. Being "saved" (*sozo*) applies to spirit, soul, and body. Jesus paid it all! No part of us is outside the reach of his redemption. Christ redeemed our whole lives with the intention that these whole lives bring him praise in greater and greater measure.

Our lives are wholly sacred, without division, because we are his. No part is left behind. Because of Christ, our lives are wholly holy.

Christ has not only made our lives holy, but he also modeled how to live out this holy cohesion during ordinary days. Tozer explains, "The Lord Jesus Christ himself is our perfect example, and he knew no divided life."[4] Though he is our great high priest, he didn't come to earth to become a priest by vocation. He became a carpenter. He worked with his very human hands to create common household items to provide for physical needs. He was born in the ordinary way (although his conception certainly wasn't ordinary) and placed in a trough amid the dung and dirt and dust kicked up from animals all around. He had all the bodily functions common to mankind. He slept. He worked. He ate. And in all of this he could rest assured, "I always do the things that are pleasing to [the Father]" (John 8:29).

Because of Christ, our lives are wholly holy.

Remember our sole vocation? It was Jesus's too. He always pleased the Father. He was never in a hurry, never fretful, frantic, or frustrated because of crowds or needs or delays. At times he got away to pray and at times he went to weddings. He lived a life of holiness because he lived a life of *wholeness*. There was no division. He entered every mundane moment as an opportunity to display the works of God, to draw attention to the Father through everything he did. He did not ignore the physical needs of those around him but, rather, met those needs and used them as a means to worship the Father and reveal the invisible realm to the watching world.

Of all the times people came to Jesus for healing, he never once responded, "You should've asked me for something more spiritual." Exactly one-hundred-percent of the time, Jesus healed them. Completely. Physically. And then he used that physical healing to point to eternal spiritual reality. Everything physical is connected to the spiritual. This entire world is an illustration. Jesus used every mundane moment as an opportunity to demonstrate the power of God in ordinary, everyday life.

Paul would later write, "Whether you eat or drink, or whatever you do, do all to the glory of God" (1 Cor. 10:31). In case we are tempted to think some things are too mundane, Paul specifically mentions eating and drinking. It gets no more mundane than these two basic human needs that transcend time and culture. We are bound by bodies we must feed multiple times a day. In fact, the Last Supper was just that—supper. It was an ordinary moment transformed because Jesus was there.

Could our meals be transformed if Christ was there? If we let him in? What about the dish duty afterward? Could housework be holy if Christ was there?

"WOMEN'S WORK"

The truth of the sacred mundane impacts justice and gender issues as well, because the sacred/secular duality has a nasty way of trickling down into every corner of life, even into the church. How we view the different spiritual gifts, roles, and duties impacts how we value each other.

No matter how many letters we have after our name, no matter how many figures in our income, no matter how far women have risen from the fetters of the 1950s housewife, someone still has to do the dishes. Right? Feminist scholar Kathleen Norris hits the nail on the head:

> Educating women is meant to free us from being relegated to such thoroughly domestic roles, and it does. But the daily we have always with us, a nagging reminder that the dishes must be done, the floor mopped or vacuumed, the dirty laundry washed. If we have grown in professional status so as to be busy with more important matters, or simply if we have enough money, we can shove the problem aside, which usually means hiring other women to do it—women who may be grateful to be employed, because they need the pay. All too often, however, we stigmatize such work as "menial," considering domestic or janitorial work

to be suitable only for those who are too limited mentally to find employment elsewhere. Cleaning up after others, or even ourselves, is not what we educate our children to do; it's for someone else's children, the less intelligent, less educated and less well-off.[5]

There is a tragedy expressed here so profound it affects the dignity of all the world's daughters and the personhood of all the world's poor. The fact that we have elevated certain tasks as more holy, sacred, or meaningful to us and God means we have relegated the majority of humankind into the ether of expendability. Only a small step exists between someone's work being considered beneath ours and someone's worth being considered beneath ours.

Only a small step exists between someone's work being considered beneath ours and someone's worth being considered beneath ours.

If we Christ followers have made that step, how are we to give his hope to the world? It is hard enough for a woman to persevere at a monotonous and mundane job, but to imply that her work is meaningless and doesn't matter strips the last shred of dignity from a precious soul whom God has called his own.

Do you see it? When we divide and devalue the life God has given us, we divide and devalue the *lives* God has given as well. Could this mindset be more widespread than we think? Could the same slithering serpent found in slavery also be found in seminary? Does only religious work please God? If our sole vocation is to please one Master, whom else are we seeking to impress? Is the church stage closer to God's presence than the nursery? What about that spot on the floor at the base of the toilet, the grossest spot I hate to scrub? Is he there? Could you worship there?

I've spent entire semesters debating whether women can be "senior pastors" (a title never mentioned in the Bible). Never once has someone asked if women should be allowed to scrub toilets. I've seen pastors jockey pathetically for position. Few give so much effort to doing dishes in their homes. We Christian authors and speakers scrap and scramble, trying to build a "platform for ministry." But ministry is serving—that is, *bowing low*. No need for a stage in order to do that.

Scripture clearly warns against elevating certain gifts above others, against clamoring for the visible ones or devaluing the private ones. Sisters, please hear my heart: I am all for empowering women to exercise their God-given gifts in ways that give him glory. I speak on stages too. But we have put on the drunk goggles and believed the world's message of what is really worthy. My work hidden in the shadows is just as valuable as that done in the spotlight. Humility is the only path to glory. Perhaps if we bowed low he'd lift us up (1 Peter 5:6).

The temptation is to believe the lie that in order to walk in greatness we must ditch the binding shackles of domestic work or dreary duties and push our way into higher realms. We've missed the point that all of life is sacred. Instead of dipping down deep into our days, we've sought escape, thinking a spiritual day spa will do more good than the filthy waters of ordinary life. The tragic fruit is our fragmented and frustrated lives. When we insist on participating in those supposedly more spiritual acts, we indicate by our choices that the stuff we're already doing—the everyday stuff—doesn't matter.

The truth is simple, and it sets us free: everything matters.

------- ❧ -------

The truth is simple, and it sets us free: everything matters.

Precious sisters, we have done this to ourselves. We—the ones who have been oppressed and exploited, left out and overlooked—have unknowingly turned on ourselves and, in our religious fervor, driven the nails into our own coffins.

Because duality brings only death to our souls. While we've worked diligently for decades to do away with the division of labor, we should have been doing away with a division of *life*. In all our efforts to break free from the mundane, we've missed the very means God provides for our transformation. The mundane is where ministry happens, where worship happens, where transformation happens. By seeking freedom from mundanity, we've missed the truth that sets us free: everything matters. We're avoiding the waters where healing is found. We've been captured by escape. And the only way to be free is to engage.

ENGAGE

We clicked the garage-door opener and heard the motor whirring, but nothing moved. We tried again. Same. We could hear sound. There was power. Energy was being expended, but that garage door was going nowhere. When we looked closer we saw the problem: the chain had slipped off the gear, so although the motor was running, nothing was moving. If gears aren't engaged, they're just spinning wheels.

The same is true in our sacred mundane. Naaman had to get in the water to be healed. He couldn't stand off and think healing thoughts. There was no way to get out of the ordeal dry. He had to enter in.

We can go through the motions of our mundane lives without truly engaging, without entering in with our whole heart, mind, and attention. But that isn't how we are healed, and it's not how we're transformed. If we don't *engage* with the gears of life, nothing will happen. We won't move forward. We'll be left spinning our wheels, completely unchanged.

Only by diving, like Naaman, into whatever dirty waters are before us will we discover that the sentence of our lives is being gloriously rewritten, right before our eyes. Once again, it's an invitation. *Come! Jump in!*

The trick is, engaging with life means embracing tension. There is contact and conflict. It's work. From an energy-output standpoint it is much easier to stand back and escape, avoid the conflict, keep a happy distance from difficulty. It takes virtually no effort to spin bicycle wheels that are up in the air. But put those wheels down on asphalt, then settle our whole weight onto that bike, and the effort needed to pedal is far greater.

But the result is much better: we move.

Friend, I don't want you stuck. I don't believe you want to be stuck, spinning your spiritual wheels up in the air, going nowhere at all. I believe that deep down, more than you desire comfort or ease or even happiness today, you want transformation. I believe you want unshakable joy. I believe you want freedom. I believe you want the sentence of your life to forever change. You should want this! It is a hunger God has put in every person. We deeply long to be all that he created us to be. We sense the holy potential. Sure, it gets warped some by the world. We're all susceptible to turning self-ward. But the truth is, you were destined for greatness. You were created to play a sacred role in the epic story of God, and the enemy wants to keep you bound in fruitless cycles of escape, spinning your wheels, standing on the shore bone dry.

The enemy wants to keep you bound in fruitless cycles of escape, spinning your wheels, standing on the shore bone dry.

Come dive in, dear friend. Get wet.

I understand the waters you're looking at probably aren't gloriously refreshing. I get that no one stands in line to swim in a swamp. We pull back, escape, or struggle to engage because, if we can be honest, these waters seem gross. Sometimes they are incredibly painful. We're tempted to step over them, or to find another path so we don't have to trudge down into them completely. It's different for each of us, but we usually know right off the bat what it is we'd rather avoid. If we could click *delete* on that aspect of life, we would. But it is precisely this aspect that teems with potential for the transformation of our hearts. The wish-we-could-change-it part of life is the key to the wish-we-could-change-it part of *ourselves*.

Just this moment, as I typed those words, a text popped up from my man. He just got out of a difficult meeting with another pastor. It involved confrontation and conflict, basically the least pleasant things ever. He said it started well but then turned TERRIBLE (yes, he used caps). But they both stuck with it, stayed engaged, and refused to give up, check out, or escape, and the meeting turned around and ended beautifully. Both men were sharpened, encouraged, and changed just a bit through the process. Yes! That is exactly it. Whether it's plunging our hands into the dishwater with enthusiasm, or diving into a project with passion, or sticking with a hard conversation by humbly listening and seeking to understand the other, life gives us daily opportunities to engage, to enter in with *hupomone* that refuses to give up, check out, or pull back. This is how we get unstuck. This is how we move. This is how we change.

And then, wonder of wonders, we start to see our environment change as well. When we dip into the water, the ripples reach the world.

MAKE CONTACT

More often than not, the dirty waters we struggle to enter involve people. Sure, some women truly despise domestic work, but most frequently the thing we seek to escape is a difficult relationship. We'll dive into this topic at length in the next chapter, but for now let's consider how *engaging* not only changes us but changes others as well. When we choose to enter in, like a moving gear coming into contact with a stationary cog, we are able to move others along as well.

I first saw this dynamic at work when my son was three. I was frustrated by his sour attitude upon waking up. It was like he woke angry at the world. (Perhaps drunk goggles materialize at a young age!) To combat this, every morning I would shower him with cheerfulness. Wanting our home's atmosphere to be one of joy, I refused to let his morning mood set the tone. With my best, widest smile and most enthusiastic voice I'd greet him every day, "Good morning, Dutch!"

He'd scowl. I'd close my eyes and pray for patience. For a long time this went on. I could effectively modify his behavior by forcing him to speak the obligatory words, "Good morning," but nothing could remove his inner grumpy-gloom. My strategy, then, was to prove that I could be more cheerful than he was grumpy—to overcome evil with good. I would smile bigger. Make my voice lighter. Greet him more enthusiastically. By golly, I was going to be happy if it killed me, and then he'd catch on and do the same. Right?

Wrong. The happier I acted, the grumpier he got. Obviously, I was missing something. It was *empathy*. That one little word changed my perspective and my life. See, it *is* our responsibility to impact the environment around us. But how do we go about that? I realized the only way to change my son was to engage with his gears. How would I do that? By getting down and locking myself in to where he was in the moment. Empathy involves entering into the feelings and emotions of another. It is to "rejoice with those who rejoice, weep with those who weep" (Rom. 12:15 NASB).

I did an experiment. The next morning, I lovingly ignored him. I gave him a quick kiss on the top of the head and said, "Hey, babe," in an off-handed, low-key way, then just let him be. To my amazement, he shuffled around the house quietly for a few minutes, then came and looked up at me with sleepy eyes.

"Mommy, I love you so much."

Was it really that simple? Could it be that my morning monster just needed a little space? A little empathy? Of course, we cannot enter into sinful behavior. This doesn't mean we join in to gossip, filthy talk, cynicism, or negativity. We are called to pull people out of the pit and up into joy. But before we can pull them up, we must first make contact and lock in to where they are now. We must empathize by entering into the thoughts, feelings, and emotions they are presently having. Unless the gears engage, they just spin.

Years later, I've seen the magic of engaged empathy work wonders with my son again and again. And while it's glorious to see him changed, it's equally amazing to see my own heart transformed as well. A decade of dipping down into those waters has changed me for good.

Friends, this is how we are transformed: not by escaping dreary domestic duties or difficult relationships, and not by dreading the daily grind or grimly bearing these weary days until we can fly away to some celestial shore. We are transformed by *engaging* in the here, the now, the conflict, the tension, letting God change us from the inside out.

This doesn't mean we don't ever hire housekeepers, pursue our God-given dreams, or use our spiritual gifts and continue attempting great things for God. It does mean we don't despise the dailiness, and we honor and esteem all people, who are created in the image of God. It means we ditch the drunk goggles, look through God's lens, and define greatness his way. We quit clawing our way up the ladder and instead bow low on the bottom rung, washing the feet of the world he loves. And we believe him when he says the greatest one is the servant of all. Nothing was beneath Jesus, so nothing is beneath us. Let's ask our humble King to help us dip down into those dirty waters, to help us engage and enter in.

5

EMBRACE: Love the One

There are no ordinary people. You have never talked to a mere mortal.
—C. S. Lewis, *The Weight of Glory*

WHEN MY SON TOLD me he loved reading about immorals, you'd better believe my ears perked up. Come again? He was curled up on the couch with the Classic Starts version of *The Iliad*. I slid in next to him. "What exactly do you mean, love?"

"You know, Odysseus, Athena, Zeus. The immorals."

Ahhh. Relieved sigh.

I snuggled a little closer and told him how happy I was that he enjoyed Greek mythology so much, then gently reminded him about the missing *t*. Indeed, *immortals* are fascinating. And every person on the planet is one.

The heart of the sacred mundane is the truth that everything matters. Because we are God's holy children, everything we do takes on sacred significance. However, to be clear, not everything matters as much.

As we celebrate the ordinary details of life, we must keep the big picture in mind. The sacred mundane is more than just feeling enthusiastic about our domestic duties. It is more than having increased joy and purpose in our daily lives. God created us for relationship with him; he came to earth to seek and save the lost. His purpose is to gather to himself a people who will worship and love him forever. This is the mission of God.

There is eternal significance to your daily, mundane duties because it is through them that you and those around you are drawn into relationship with God. The house you keep, the car you drive, the physical body you inhabit, the time you manage, the money in your wallet, all these things will eventually pass away. The only thing that will last for eternity is the eternal human soul.

And you are surrounded by eternal souls. Immortals. Everything matters because of how much people matter. C. S. Lewis said it like this: "There are no ordinary people. You have never talked to a mere mortal. Nations, cultures, arts, civilization—these are mortal, and their life is to ours as the life of a gnat. But it is immortals whom we joke with, work with, marry, snub, and exploit—immortal horrors or everlasting splendors. . . . Next to the Blessed Sacrament itself, your neighbor is the holiest object presented to your senses."[1]

Do you see why the mundane is so sacred? It is populated with immortals. The cashier, the postal worker, your husband and children, your friends and enemies, your mother-in-law, and your neighbor, these are eternal beings, all traveling through life toward one of two eternal destinations. That is why everything matters.

The cashier, the postal worker, your husband and children . . . these are eternal beings.

My kids have asked if there are toys in heaven. I sometimes wonder if the beautiful trees and mountains, rivers, lakes, valleys—if all these glorious creations will be part of the new earth. Probably. I don't know. But I do know two things that will for sure be there: God and people. Our mundane activities carry eternal significance when we consider those two things: God and people. Yes, there are many commands in the Bible, but Jesus said the greatest is this: "'Love the Lord your God with all your heart and with all your soul and with all your mind.' This is the first and greatest commandment. And the second is like it: 'Love your neighbor as yourself.' All the Law and the Prophets hang on these two commandments" (Matt. 22:37–40 NIV).

Paul makes it clear that *all* the commandments "are summed up in this word: 'You shall love your neighbor as yourself.' Love does no wrong to a neighbor; therefore love is the fulfilling of the law" (Rom. 13:9–10). Later he tells us that "the whole law is fulfilled in one word: 'You shall love your neighbor as yourself'" (Gal. 5:14).

This is what really matters. Everything hangs on this. Everything else matters only in its relation to this. Because of the glory of God and the potential glory of every individual, our lives carry eternal weight. We're always helping others along toward one of two destinations.

Now, as I write those words I understand I am going to lose some of you. You might even put this book down, writing me off as one of those fire-and-brimstone crazies who stands on the street corner telling people to "turn or burn."

I'm not. But I do believe in two distinct eternal destinations for every human soul. Scripture clearly teaches this, and without the weight of this reality, we're just playing house. Please hear my heart in this: life is not a game. We're not just warming up for the real thing. As much as we've been emphasizing that this world is temporary, that we need to look through it to the eternal realm, we must not therefore disengage from the reality of this physical world, especially the sacred souls who inhabit it.

Quite frankly, if the afterlife that Jesus promised isn't real, we're just wasting our time. Paul said, "If our hope in Christ is only for this life, we are more to be pitied than anyone in the world" (1 Cor. 15:19 NLT). The Christian life doesn't make a lick of sense without the very present hope and reality of eternal life. Erase this doctrine and the cross of Christ is wholly unnecessary. We will never understand the sacredness of every mundane moment until we understand the weight of eternity.

But as C. S. Lewis has said, this doesn't make us "perpetually solemn." The most profound joy and lightness isn't found in triviality and flippancy but in rightly esteeming others as made in God's image, with glorious potential far beyond what we can see.

We take life seriously but ourselves not too much. God is God. This is his world. It's his gig. His story. And he's graciously invited us to join him with every breath we breathe. Everything matters, but the heart of this always, always revolves around relationship. Radical, relational love is the very heart of the gospel.

THE HEART OF THE GOSPEL

For many years I taught that the heart of the gospel is grace. And it is, sort of. But what motivates grace? Love. We show grace—unmerited favor—to another person because of love. Love is always what motivates grace, and love is what motivated the greatest act of grace of all time—the gift of Jesus Christ, the sacrifice for our sins. Love is the heart of the gospel.

But what is love?

We must ditch the world's drunk goggles and define love the way God does—and God defines love by the cross of Christ. A picture is worth a thousand words, right? God skips the lengthy definitions and paints us a picture instead, with his own blood. He makes love manifest, makes it clear for all to see. "In this the love of God was made manifest among us, that God sent his only Son into the world, so that we might live through him. In this is love, not that we have loved God but that he loved us and sent his Son to be the propitiation for our sins" (1 John 4:9–10).

If we want to know how best to love others, we just look to Jesus. I know this seems elementary, but often we forget. We find ourselves seeking advice from every source but the Source. We take our relational woes to everyone but him. We read every advice column except the one in Scripture. We turn to self-help, but we need his help.

The real problem is, Jesus's kind of love is terribly inconvenient. Jesus's kind of love is appalling. It's so far beyond our own diluted view of love, we hardly know what to do with it. He laid down all his rights—and I can barely lay down my plans for the day!

Think about it. Jesus gave up all his privileges, his comforts, his glory, his honor, his majesty, to come down and dwell among us in our filthy mess. He canceled all his plans and made *us* his plan. He came and pitched his tent among us (John 1:14). He moved into our neighborhood. He didn't come and live in a palace. He didn't come as an earthly king. He wasn't more handsome than everyone else. He didn't have a holy glow about him; he wasn't a head taller than everyone else. There was nothing about his person or appearance that would make him attractive to us (Isa. 53:2). Jesus was born into a poor family. Before his three-and-a-half years of itinerant ministry, he worked a mundane job as a humble carpenter.

And he lived the most others-centered, selfless, loving, giving, sacrificial life that could ever be conceived. Jesus lived the life we should live but don't. And he laid down his life for us, reconciling us back to the Father, rescuing us and bringing us into the family of God. He took all our sin and shame, our envy and hate, our greed and selfishness. The sinless Lamb of God, Jesus, bore the punishment for our sin so that we wouldn't have to. His love was immeasurably costly.

It cost him everything.

The love that Jesus demonstrated brings me to my knees. And not in a neat and tidy way. In an undone way. In a "Woe is me!" way. His love is so incredibly over the top that it messes with us to the core. We desperately try to devise ways to intelligently explain away the biblical obligation to live out this kind of love. Because Jesus's love is mind-blowing, and to love others in this way seems an impossible goal. Where do we even begin?

THIMBLEFULS

Jesus clarifies the kind of love with which we are to love others. He says, "A new commandment I give to you, that you love one another: *just as I have loved you*, you also are to love one another" (John 13:34, emphasis mine). Again, in John 15:12, Jesus says, "This is my commandment, that you love one another as I have loved you." The apostle John wrote, "Beloved, if God so loved us, we also ought to love one another" (1 John 4:11). It is the transformative love of God that compels us to love others: "We love because he first loved us" (1 John 4:19; see also 2 Cor. 5:14).

This kind of love, the Jesus kind of love, seems impossible for us to embody. How can we even come close to loving others to the extent that Christ has loved them? Not a chance. But we are to love with the same kind of love—the same substance, if you will. If Christ's love for us is the vast ocean, we are to love others with a thimbleful of that same ocean water.

If Christ's love for us is the vast ocean, we are to love others with a thimbleful of that same ocean water.

This means that even if it's an itty-bitty love offering, it's Christ's kind of love. It's the kind that never gives up, that cares more for others than for self, that doesn't want what it doesn't have. It's the kind that doesn't strut, doesn't have a swelled head, doesn't force itself on others. It's the love that isn't always "me first," that doesn't fly off the handle or keep score of the sins of others. This love doesn't revel when others grovel but takes pleasure in the flowering of truth. This love "puts up with anything, trusts God always, always looks for the best, never looks back, but keeps going to the end" (1 Cor. 13:7 MSG).

This is the stuff. Let's pour out little thimblefuls of this. The simplest way to sum up this kind of love is found in 1 John 3:16, "By this we know love, that he laid down his life for us, and we ought to lay down our lives for the brothers."

Life laid down: this is the essence of Christ's kind of love. "Greater love has no one than this, that someone lay down his life for his friends" (John 15:13). This is the greatest love, the love we have come to know and believe (1 John 4:16). This love is what we get to offer daily to our desperate world.

HOW LOVE BECOMES REAL

Christ clothed himself in skin, the real kind, in order to make clear to us what the love of the Father is like. What was spoken to us abstractly was shown to us concretely through the person of Jesus Christ. He made love real for us.

So, how does our love become real? When my children were little, one of their favorite stories was *The Velveteen Rabbit*. The alternate title for this classic children's book is *How Toys Become Real*. Clearly the former title is more memorable, but I like the latter as well because it captures exactly what the heart of the story really is. How do toys become real?

Love. Toys become real when they are loved on by a real child, petted and propped up and dragged around by the ears. By being snuggled under the covers and thrown up in the air. And when all the fur wears off and an eye falls off and a stitch or two becomes loose . . . then a toy is real.

Our love becomes real in a similar way when it rubs up against real people. When the abstract becomes concrete and we're dragged around a bit. When our fur wears off and we lose our polished appearance.

Jesus made love real for us by walking in the dirt, right by our side. Not only that, but he focused on a few people so they could see specific examples of love lived out. Although Jesus demonstrated his love for all humanity, I'm always fascinated by his love displayed through his relationship with the apostle John. John was the one who wrote, "Let us not love in word or talk but in deed and in truth" (1 John 3:18). I believe John understood better than anyone how real love works because he was the closest disciple to Christ. John witnessed when love came to town, and he found himself front and center for the greatest display of true love the world had ever seen.

See, because Jesus was bound by an earthly body, he could not equally pour out his attention on all people. He daily faced the same time and attention limitations as we do. I often feel frustrated because so many people want me at once. Imagine how Jesus felt with crowds clamoring for his attention! Yet in the midst of it, Jesus often chose to give focused attention to John.

John was the disciple who leaned against Jesus's chest at dinner. He was with Jesus on the Mount of Transfiguration, he was (ahem) sleeping in the garden of Gethsemane during Jesus's final hours, and he was at the foot of the cross when all the other disciples fled. Among the multitudes, the seventy-two, the twelve, and the three, John was the one.

Because of this, I always turn to John when I want the real scoop on what Jesus's love is like. John knew the importance of narrowing it down to "the one" because he had experienced *being* "the one." He uses this simple but powerful strategy of focusing in on the individual in his epistles. For instance, in 1 John 3:16 he's telling us to lay down our lives for our brothers. But then, in the very next verse, John narrows it down to the one: "If anyone has the world's goods and sees his brother in need, yet closes his heart against him, how does God's love abide in him?" Instead of using the plural, "the brothers," he moves to the singular form, "his brother."

Track with me here. If we need to know how to really love people in our daily lives, how to embrace the immortal souls God has entrusted to our care, we have to focus in on the one. Our love is only as real as it is to a single person. C. S. Lewis said it like this: "It is easier to be enthusiastic about Humanity with a capital 'H' than it is to love individual men and women, especially those who are uninteresting, exasperating, depraved, or otherwise unattractive. Loving everybody in general may be an excuse for loving nobody in particular."[2]

Ha! Only C. S. Lewis can talk like that! But isn't it true? My son loves to quote Charlie Brown's friend Linus: "I love humanity. It's people I can't stand!" It's so much easier to be enthusiastic about loving "humanity"—a group of people, an abstract idea. But if we don't love the single person God has put in front of us, we don't truly love. Love is lived out with the real people whom God has sovereignly placed in our lives. Love becomes real by embracing the one.

THE ONE

This focusing in on "the one" is the same teaching technique Jesus used. In the tenth chapter of Luke, when a lawyer stood up to test Jesus about how to inherit eternal life, Jesus turned his attention to the Law. The lawyer rattled off the commandments—clearly he had this stuff down pat. Jesus basically said, "Great, do this and you'll live."

Pregnant pause. I can almost see the wheels turning in the mind of that lawyer: *Love your neighbor as . . . hmm . . . what about* that *person? Do I actually have to love* him? *I'd better clarify.* The lawyer clears his throat, perhaps trying to act nonchalant: "Um . . . who exactly is my neighbor?" (vv. 25–29).

I don't know if Jesus smiled then, but I always imagine he did. He knew the heart of the lawyer, and he loved him. He also knows how desperately we all want to justify our own behavior. God knows how we'll go to any length to feel okay about the way we're already living. And he loves us still. Jesus replies with the well-known story of the good Samaritan.

God knows how we'll go to any length to feel okay about the way we're already living. And he loves us still.

"A man was going down from Jerusalem to Jericho, and he fell among robbers, who stripped him and beat him and departed, leaving him half dead. Now by chance a priest was going down that road, and when he saw him he passed by on the other side. So likewise a Levite, when he came to the place and saw him, passed by on the other side. But a Samaritan, as he journeyed, came to where he was, and when he saw him, he had compassion. He went to him and bound up his wounds, pouring on oil and wine. Then he set him on his own animal and brought him to an inn and took care of him. And the next day he took out two denarii and gave them to the innkeeper, saying, 'Take care of him, and whatever more you spend, I will repay you when I come back.' Which of these three, do you think, proved to be a neighbor to the man who fell among the robbers?" He said, "The one who showed him mercy." And Jesus said to him, "You go, and do likewise." (Luke 10:30–37)

When Jesus wanted to help the lawyer's love become real, he directed him to the one. What the Samaritan did was simple. We laud him as a hero, which he is, but his heroism is rather regular. He was simply walking along the road, and there was "the one" in front of him. Instead of avoiding the need as the priest and Levite had done, he stopped. He stooped. He used what he had in order to embrace the one. He helped the man onto his animal, took him to an inn, and paid for all the necessary provisions. We could say he *looked* with eyes of love, *listened* to the Holy Spirit with a humble heart, *engaged* and entered into the mess in front of him, and *embraced* the one whom Providence had placed in his path.

This is how we dip down deep into our days. And Jesus said this is how we love our neighbor, thus fulfilling the Law and the Prophets. Could it really be this simple?

Perhaps real love is this: a willingness to stop, stoop, and embrace the one whom Providence places in our path.

PENIELLE

In chapter 1, I mentioned Penielle. That isn't her real name, but the Hebrew word *Peniel* means "face of God" in Genesis 32:30, and it reminds me that the "least of these" are Jesus in disguise (see Matt. 25:31–45), and that we behold the face of God when we look into the eyes of the poor.

Meeting Penielle was actually an answer to a desperate prayer. I prayed it about six months into planting a church, when I was discouraged. Actually discouraged doesn't begin to describe how I was feeling. I was overwhelmed with hopelessness. Our little fledgling congregation was barely limping along. Our gatherings were awkward at best, excruciating at worst. Several church services felt like such a circus that I almost vowed never to return. (Of course, when you're the pastor's wife, you kind of have to attend.)

But it wasn't the state of the church that most discouraged me. It was the state of my heart. What God revealed to me was that all of my issues and frustrations boiled down to my own heart condition. Quite frankly, I didn't love people.

Well, I loved some people. Many! But then there were others. And these others seemed to be coming to our church in an alarmingly high concentration. I wanted to please the Father, but I was struggling with doubt and discouragement, wondering if I was cut out for this whole church-planting thing.

One day, in one ordinary moment, as I stood at my kitchen counter, a desperate plea came straight from my heart, whispered into the silence: *Please, God—teach me to love.*

Please, God—teach me to love.

It wasn't the kind of poetic prayer you deliver at a prayer meeting. It was the helpless cry of a dying soul. I desperately needed help truly loving people.

The next day, one of my kids called in from the other room: "Mommy! There's a little boy on our porch!"

I came to the window. Sure enough, a little boy was playing on our front porch. There's a bus stop there as well, so I craned my neck and on the bottom step sat a woman smoking a cigarette. My internal Missional Opportunity Alert went off.

"Come on, kids! Let's go say hello!"

We went out and said hello. The mom, Penielle, seemed agitated and out of breath. As we began to talk, more and more things just didn't seem right. I had no experience with drug abuse, but clearly something was awry. She wound up missing the bus because we were talking, so she asked if I could please give her and her son a ride home. I couldn't at that moment, but I invited her and her son in for a while.

I let her in.

As she walked across the front door threshold, she stopped, mid stride, looking up. "What is that? It's so . . . *light*. It's like something just lifted off my chest. It's like, I've never felt this before. It's just so . . . *light*." I believed her that something had lifted off her chest, and I hoped it wasn't now flying around my house!

I had no idea then how that visit would impact everything. Details aren't necessary, but the next thing Jeff and I knew, we were caught up in a whirlwind of police calls, DHS trips, court hearings, adoption training, and jail visits. My neat-and-tidy life in which I had struggled to love slightly challenging people seemed a distant dream. God had placed "the one" on my doorstep, a mix of mental illness, drug abuse, and demonic oppression . . . a beautiful and broken daughter of God who desperately needed love. And here I was, another beautiful and broken daughter of God who desperately needed *to* love.

He had answered my prayer.

Helping Penielle was like standing on the edge of a vast black hole. I was terrified. I had no experience with drug addiction, abuse, severe mental illness, or the court system. For six months we stumbled along together, Jeff and I learning by trial and error (mostly error) how to help Penielle best. Eventually she completed an inpatient drug treatment program. Then when she got out, she called us.

"You're the only people I know who aren't on drugs. Can I live with you?"

God taught me to love by stripping me of control.

I just happened to be studying 1 John 3:16–18 when she called. Remember what I said in chapter 3 about liking my space, my quiet? We already had a housemate, and Penielle would officially make a full house. I could feel myself dying inside as the last little bit of control slipped from my fingertips. Letting her in would officially make my life unmanageable.

In the most glorious sense.

God taught me to love by stripping me of control. I could manage my home, my schedule, my children. I couldn't manage Penielle. She absolutely baffled me. But as I laid her request before the Lord, as I posed the possibility to Jeff, and as we prayed together about it, we were reminded again and again of 1 John 3:17. As best we knew how, we *looked* at the world through God's Word: "If anyone has the world's goods and sees his brother in need, yet closes his heart against him, how does God's love abide in him?"

Really, all the Good Samaritan did was not avoid the person Providence had placed in his path. He simply took what he had and shared it with another in need. How could we ignore this verse? Hard as I tried, I just couldn't make it say anything other than what it says.

There were plenty of things we should have done before inviting Penielle into our home. They would have enabled all of us to be more successful. But God was graciously giving us a hands-on lab at this life lesson, and although we didn't ace every test, that wasn't the point. We were learning to *embrace* and love the one.

After five months living together, God in his providence moved Penielle on and out of our home. We still stay in touch and I love her dearly, but she's no longer under our roof. I remember the day she moved out. I cleaned out her bedroom and sat down, feeling both sad and relieved, thinking we could now go back to regular life. That same day I received a text from a friend: "I have a homeless gal here who needs a place to stay. Do you have room?"

My eyes widened in wonder. "Wait, Lord: This is a thing?"

I could almost hear the Father chuckling. *Yes, dear child, this is a thing.* This "loving people" is a thing if there ever was one. "The one" will change with each season of life, but there will always be one. Later we had the privilege of welcoming another Penielle. At thirty-six, she'd been on heroin and worked as a prostitute for twenty years.

Today we have a whole different set of housemates who are pure joy, so "the one" looks like something different in this season.

See, sometimes the one is a coworker, an in-law, one of your children, even your spouse. The one is whomever God has sovereignly placed in your path, plunked down on your doorstep, so to speak: the person he is empowering you to love even when it's hard. He or she is your "Penielle," where you will see the face of God. The one is the answer to your own heart's prayer, *Teach me to love.* Whether you've voiced that petition or not, the Father knows we need to embrace and love the one in order to fathom more fully his limitless love for us.

This is how love becomes real. This kind of love cannot be learned from a distance. Remember *The Velveteen Rabbit*? How his fur wore off and an eye fell off and a stitch or two came loose? This happens through contact. We can well-wish at arm's length, but we cannot love this way. This love doesn't veer to the other side of the road and shout over its shoulder, "Be warm and filled!" This love is an embrace.

> This love doesn't veer to the other side of the road and shout over
> its shoulder, "Be warm and filled!" This love is an embrace.

Now, I don't want to sugarcoat this: our experience with Penielle was painful. But it prepared the way for other ongoing relationships. It made me open up to other opportunities. It enlarged the place of our tent and stretched out the curtains of our habitation. It helped us to not hold back but lengthen our cords and strengthen our stakes (Isa. 54:2). I had often prayed that prayer, thinking of God giving me more influence through writing and speaking. Instead he stretched our food budget and filled our bedrooms. We are the ones blessed.

YOU ARE ONLY ONE

Part of learning to love meant learning that just because I embrace the one doesn't mean I am the only one to do so. In fact, I am *only* one, not *the* only one. Here's what I mean: I believe some of what made the situation with Penielle turn sour was that I overhelped. The epiphany came when a wise friend said, "You're working very hard to help Penielle. I just hope you're not working harder to help Penielle than *Penielle* is working to help Penielle."

I received her admonishment. It was true. I was constantly swooping in to help, responding to Penielle's begging, rescuing her from situations. I loved her very much. I wanted her to succeed. (Idol alert! More on that in a moment.) But I was doing too much of the work. I am only one, and I was doing the work of two. Actually, I was doing the work of twenty. I should have helped but not overreached. When we finally began allowing Penielle to experience her own painful consequences, she was livid because she felt like we were pulling away.

Later, as I returned to Jesus's parable, I noticed that the Good Samaritan didn't make the injured man his lifelong project. He didn't adopt him into his home. He didn't even stay at the inn. He recognized that he was only one. There were others who would enter into this story and help the man as well. And, the wounded man would play a part too. The Good Samaritan simply offered what he had, paid for all the necessary provisions, then went on his way. There was a freedom to give and help without feeling compelled to do it all himself. He was only one, and he was not the only one who could help.

There is tremendous peace in knowing we are often called into someone's life only for a season. Pride pushes us to do it all ourselves, but this only ends in a swollen ego (when the person succeeds) or despair (when the person fails). When I am prompted to lovingly let go, I can humbly trust that another Christian brother or sister will step in for the next season. People are never projects to complete. Our work continues then through intercession, and we can genuinely rejoice when another gets to reap the results. We can secretly rejoice with our Father that he allowed us to be part of the process. This is joy!

I don't share this in order to excuse anyone from extended periods of service. I don't regret bringing Penielle or anyone else into our home. I simply share this to remind us that part of loving well is loving wisely. Jesus offered the gift of salvation to all who would listen, but he never chased people down and begged them to accept. When someone did not want to respond, Jesus moved on. This doesn't mean we write people off, but we cling closer to God than to whomever we're serving. God's Word must be our wisdom, his voice our constant guide.

Loving well and wisely in this way must flow out of the confident security of knowing I am a child of God. Our identity is firmly in him; it can never become tied up in what we do. Someone else's success or failure does not establish our worth. If we seek to find our identity and satisfaction in anything other than the unconditional love of God, our efforts to love will inevitably fall flat. An unstable heart will quickly construct an idol, which becomes the saboteur of real love.

LOVE'S SABOTEUR

John concludes his epistle on love with this surprising statement: "Little children, keep yourselves from idols" (1 John 5:21). It seems out of place, this interjection about idolatry, when the theme has been sacrificial love. But in reality it's perfectly placed, for John understood that idolatry will sabotage our earnest efforts to love.

John understood that idolatry will sabotage our earnest efforts to love.

In Deuteronomy 5:7, we read the first commandment: "You shall have no other gods before me." Many scholars say that this commandment actually encapsulates all the other commandments in one. If we get number one, we get them all. When Jesus came on the scene and distilled all the Law and the Prophets into one, he said we were to love God and our neighbor. In short, when other gods are gone, love is present. When other gods are present, love is not. Idolatry is love's saboteur.

Now, most of us don't have golden calves in our homes, so what are these idols I speak of? Idols are simply the false gods of this world that we unknowingly bow to when we mindlessly meander in the course of this world (Eph. 2:2). John Calvin said the human heart is a factory of idols,[3] and unfortunately there is no limit to the types we can manufacture.

In *The Gospel Primer* Caesar Kalinowski identifies the four main idols of the heart that most often lure us away from love—comfort, approval, control, and success. For each, he pinpoints the negative results of these idols and how they affect those around us:

COMFORT: An idol of *comfort* makes us crave privacy, a lack of stress, and freedom from responsibility. We fear being burdened or tied down by demands. Enslaved to comfort, we sacrifice productivity, and others often feel hurt because of our unwillingness to sacrifice our needs or wants for the sake of others. We battle boredom because we're not willing to risk the stress that may accompany ventures of faith.

APPROVAL: An idol of *approval* makes us slaves to others' affirmation, love, and attention. We have an excessive need for relationship, and rejection is our greatest nightmare. We give up confidence and independence in a desperate effort to win acceptance. Our loved ones often feel smothered, sensing that too much rides on their response to us, and we cower in fear because we can't stand the thought of losing others' approval.

CONTROL: An idol of *control* drives us to self-discipline, decisiveness, and high standards. We avoid uncertainty or situations that feel chaotic. Bound by control, we often feel lonely, sacrificing spontaneity and flexibility because we can't release our high need for control. Those around us often feel judged or condemned by our unyielding expectations, and we battle anxiety about the—inevitable—situations outside our control.

SUCCESS: An idol of *success* lures us ever higher to power, winning, and increased influence. Fear of failure and humiliation is enough to keep us striving onward, even if we feel crushed by the burden of responsibility we carry. Those around us sometimes feel used, sensing our greatest aim is our own achievements, and we often struggle with anger when others get in our way or we cannot attain what we so desperately want.[4]

We struggle to love others when they get in the way of our idol. When we have the idol of *comfort* and someone in our life demands things of us that strip us of that comfort, we get stressed and mad. When we have an idol of *approval* and someone is not giving us approval—withholding it, not extending friendship, rejecting us—we reel. We cannot forgive them;

we struggle to love them. When we have an idol of *control* and something or someone throws everything into chaos—when things spin out of our plans and our control, we become anxious—we struggle to love whoever threw our life off-kilter. When we worship *success* and someone humiliates us or makes us feel like a failure, we find it hard to love that person.

When Jeff and I first began our church plant, I struggled to enjoy the people God had entrusted to us because I was unknowingly seeking an idol of success. When God smashed that idol, he freed me up to love people. Now I can honestly say I am free to enjoy every person who comes (or leaves) our church, because my identity isn't tied up in the success of this thing. I'm a child of God, and I will love whomever he brings my way.

Idolatry taints our love and makes it warped, limited, and incomplete. I later recognized that the same idol of success had sabotaged my love for Penielle. I did love her, but I also wanted her to succeed. Nothing wrong with that, but *her* success became dangerously tied up (in my mind) with *my* success. I worked my tail off for her, not always out of selfless love, but because I didn't want my "project" to fail! Again, people are never projects, and our identity (and mental health!) can never be tied to the success or failure of another person. Not ever.

People are never projects.

Idolatry will sabotage love every time, so it's critical that we deal with our heart idols (again and again and again) so we can purely and freely love others. Whenever we struggle to love the one, we are wise to take a step back and honestly ask ourselves, What idol is sabotaging my love?

This is why the sacred mundane matters so much—because there are no ordinary people. Our mundane lives are packed full of immortals, eternal souls we are helping toward one destination or another. These sacred souls are what make our mundane so significant. Every commandment is summed up in one simple invitation: come, love the one. You will see the face of God, because the one is really Jesus in disguise.

6

TRUST: Live the Blank

❖———————❖———————❖

Do not fear, only believe.
—Mark 5:36

"'NOT HAVING A GOAL is more to be feared than not reaching a goal. I would rather attemt to do somtheing great and fail than attenpemt to do notheing and succeed.'—Victor Frankel"

This is exactly how I wrote it on September 6, 1989. In careful child's cursive across the top of a page, I penned this quote under the large heading: Life Goals. A Precious Moments sticker is awkwardly placed near the top left, likely where I had begun writing, messed up, and started over. Looking back, I see that not only did I spell Viktor Frankl's name incorrectly, but apparently the quote should be attributed to Robert Schuller. Oh dear. I wish I could add a laughing-tears emoji here and hashtag "homeschool."

I was nine at the time. My mom had given my brother and me four categories and asked us to write a one-sentence goal for each. Determining one's life goals at that age seems rather ambitious, but my answers clearly weren't. The page reads as follows:

God: Pray and read the Bible every day.
Family and church: Obey my parents.
Self: Save money and earn money.
World:

Fair enough. It's interesting to see how similar I am more than a quarter century later. In some ways you could summarize my current life as a simple girl with poor handwriting who prays and reads her Bible every day, obeys her parents, and saves money (I don't earn much!). My spelling has improved slightly, and I cite sources a bit more carefully, but that's about it.

I found this list in 2010 while unpacking from a move. There was nothing remarkable about the goals, but what caught my attention was what's not there. Why was the "World" goal left blank?

I don't remember writing those goals, and there's no telling what caused me to leave the assignment unfinished. What's interesting is that, up to that point, my life goal for the world had been exactly what I wrote: nothing. My vision was very much unfinished. I was faithful about reading the Bible, obeying authorities, and stewarding finances, but my passion and concern ended right about there: at the walls of my own home.

Sure, I knew that "God so loved the world." My family supported missionaries and sponsored a kid in Africa. I have family from Calcutta, Japan, and Bangladesh, so I knew the world wasn't white. I had been on numerous short-term mission trips and traveled through Europe. But a heart for the world? A love for the world? A goal for how my life impacts the world? Not at all.

I remember the day I sat there holding that rediscovered paper, light in my hands but heavy on my heart. It wasn't just a list; it was the proverbial final straw. God had been throwing countless other things my way, challenging the "normal" life I desperately wanted to live. This blank represented so much more. The weight of conviction felt crushing, pinning me down; there was no slipping out from under it. How had I gone so long without a passion for the world God died for? In that moment, I realized I'd been missing the whole point. The world: that's the point.

I looked back down at the page. It wasn't just that I didn't love the world enough. There was something else. Something very vulnerable, something deep, was touched as I looked at my list. I was struck by the simple fact that my life goals were very, very . . . safe.

Yes. That was the word. Safe. Sure, I could justify it; I was only nine at the time, for crying out loud! But the same aim-small, play-it-safe, limit-the-risks mind-set that characterized my childhood was still very much with me as an adult. Most of my life had been driven by one aim: don't mess up. It was tragic but true. Why didn't I have a goal for the world? *Who gives a rip about the world! I'm just trying to keep from making a royal mess out of each day. Isn't that enough? Can't you see I'm busting my tail just trying to behave? Who has time to reach the world? I'm just trying to read my Bible every day and please my parents!*

The quote at the top of the page said that not having a goal was more to be feared than not reaching a goal, but clearly I didn't believe it because I hadn't made a goal! The top three categories represented my comfort zone. I could "be a good Christian" and just fulfill the top three. In fact, my life passion for the sacred mundane seemed to line up well with that: stay home, keep your nose down, do the dishes, and pray a lot. Don't mess up. The end.

It was that fourth goal that pushed me far beyond the safe zone and into dangerous territory. Into the kingdom of heaven. If the God I believed in just wanted me to have a good devotional life and raise obedient kids, I was okay with that. But if the God I believed in loved the world and called his followers to dive headlong into his kingdom and care about the world he died for . . . ai yai yai! Now I'm shifting in my seat!

> Those whose deep-seated motivation is to not mess up will never, ever risk it all and go for broke for the kingdom of God.

Those whose deep-seated motivation is to not mess up will never, ever risk it all and go for broke for the kingdom of God. It's just too dangerous. Church is safe. Devotions are safe. Following the rules is safe.

Faith isn't.

Busting open that life-savings alabaster jar and pouring it on someone's feet isn't.

Giving away both mites, all you have, isn't.

Selling the farm, all you own, in order to buy an empty lot . . . isn't.

Staring at the blank in that list I had written so long ago, I closed my eyes and felt "safe" slip away. Something whispered in my heart, *Live the blank.*

SELL THE FARM

In Matthew 13:44, Jesus tells a short story that perfectly illustrates what was happening with Jeff and me. He said, "The kingdom of heaven is like treasure hidden in a field, which a man found and covered up. Then in his joy he goes and sells all that he has and buys that field." A newly discovered deal can make us do drastic things. We've all been there in some way or another. (Black Friday frenzies come to mind.) It's crazy, really, how one discovery changes everything, how it can make us do ridiculous things. I'm not exaggerating when I say that in one day, everything in our life looked radically different. It was disturbing and distressing and glorious all at once. We'd found a treasure in a field, but, alas, we didn't own it.

I had no idea how deeply and how desperately I wanted to prove, to myself and others, that I wasn't what I thought I was.

We owned plenty of other things, though: purchased representations of success. In chapter 4, I shared our four-year journey of silence and confusion. At the time, I didn't realize how that season was ingraining the word *failure* in my heart. The enemy handed it to me month after month like a nametag. Somewhere along the line I'd taken it and put it right on, believing it was my identity. I had no idea how deeply and how desperately I wanted to prove, to myself and others, that I wasn't what I thought I was.

During that season my brother landed a lucrative job, while we were jobless, penniless, and living with my parents. I still remember standing in their kitchen, hearing about his wildly successful career and hating myself because I wasn't truly happy about it. I forced a smile and choked congratulations out. I longed to genuinely celebrate others' successes. I loved my brother, but my fierce fear of failure gripped my emotions, keeping me bound. That night, as I put our son to bed, I leaned my head down on the rail of his crib and cried, whispering to God the only desperate words that would come: *Please, God. Change me.*

God did begin to change me, but the road was circuitous. A year after that difficult season ended, we found ourselves "living the dream." At least, what I thought was my dream. Jeff landed a fabulous job as an associate pastor at a large, thriving church. I was the director of women's ministry and was speaking at retreats. We had two beautiful children, health insurance, and a 401(k).

Not only that, but we'd been able to scrape together enough to build our dream home. After moving eleven times and making do with some miserable (to me) living situations, I was over the moon. Finally, a place to settle. It was truly a pinch-me situation. I chose carpet colors and cabinets, picked out tile and paint. We dreamed up floor-to-ceiling shelves to house all our beloved Bible books. This exquisite house would be the perfect place for ministry, tucked in an affluent area of our beautiful town.

The first year there, we poured hours into perfecting everything—window treatments, landscape, and a playhouse for the kids. Finally we finished. I looked around. At last I had a life that looked a little less like a complete failure. This—*this*—proved I wasn't a mess. I could be happy for others' successes now because my own success was firmly established. I distinctly remember standing at my kitchen sink and looking out the window, feeling full of "peace" and "contentment," and thinking to myself, *Ahhh! Finished.*

But something was unfinished: that yellowed paper from 1989. I discovered it the very next week as I finished up the last bit of unpacking. And everything unraveled. That silly blank was like a little domino tipped over to begin the process of completely flattening our nice, newly constructed lives.

Just when I thought I'd cleaned up my life, God made a much bigger mess of it. It was nothing less than an all-out attack on our comfort, security, peace, and happiness—launched by God himself. At least that's how it felt. Apparently, he wanted to let that success idol grow really large, house sized, before he took a sledgehammer to it. He wanted to make sure I'd tasted my dream before he showed me something infinitely better.

God amped up the assault by placing a bomb on my bookshelf: *The Hole in Our Gospel* by Richard Stearns, the president of World Vision. (Some books should come with warning labels!) It destroyed me, shattering my distorted lens of American-dream Christianity and letting me see the Scriptures in a new light.

But that wasn't all. God continued putting seriously disturbing things in my path—sermons and studies and documentaries. Where was this stuff coming from? Where had the book of James been all my life? And what was up with Isaiah 58? Had that been in there all along? Apparently the world out there was in dire need not only of gospel truth but food and clean water too. Twenty-five thousand children were dying each day of preventable causes. *They were?* Who knew?

I became the crazy lady. Did everybody else know about this? Why was it all kept a secret from me all these years? It was all I could do to keep going through the motions of each day as normal. I wanted to pound on doors and show photos of dying children in Africa. *People! Do y'all* know *about this?* I tried to be calm. I tried not to yell at people in the grocery store. I tried not to reach into their carts and wave needless items up in the air. *You don't need chewing gum, people!*

Mostly I succeeded. I didn't yell at anyone. But I did sit up at night weeping. I just had never known. I suppose I "knew" in some cerebral sense, but not in my heart. God's love for the world hadn't been poured into me in this sense before, to where it flooded over the self-love that pulses through our fallen veins. Suddenly the invisible kingdom of heaven seemed real, more real than what we saw with our physical eyes. I finally valued a starving toddler more than my travertine floors. Jeff and I suddenly saw true worth. The hidden treasure in the field was found.

It was time to sell the farm.

DITCH "SAFE"

This invisible, upside-down kingdom had been there all along, but somehow we'd missed it. We were too busy building our own kingdom—a nice, comfy, safe one. One where success is the king.

We had been believers for years. Our lives were plenty churchy. We were professional Christians, both of us got paid to teach God's truth. And yet, if we were completely honest, the trajectory of our lives was very much the trajectory of the world. In the midst of our church work, we wanted comfort, control, approval, and success. Same goals as the world's, just dressed up in churchy clothes.

I wanted a ministry job that paid well. I wanted well-behaved kids and a comfortable home. I wanted to be successful in speaking and writing. I wanted people to like me. If I was dead-bang honest, which I wasn't, I would have admitted that I'd be okay with becoming a big-name Christian author and speaker.

There you have it. My ugly pride. I know, it's disgusting. (You probably want a refund for this book now that you know the deplorable author. I don't blame you.) On the one hand it's appalling, but on the other hand, only pitiful. See, I really just wanted not to mess up. If I was painfully honest, I wanted my family to be proud of me. That was my safe life goal.

I had no heart for the world. . . . My own heart's hunger trumped world hunger every time.

That's why I had no heart for the world. There wasn't any heart left after me. My own heart's hunger trumped world hunger every time.

The truth is, the hardest thing in the world is to make my heart care about the world outside the walls of our home. Why? Because the heart's fierce effort to protect itself and feed itself keeps us bound in a life of "safe." We fear messing up so much, it keeps us locked inside.

Powered by this fear, my heart is like a magnet, pulling everything in toward me. Martin Luther said, "Sin is the heart's propensity to curve in on itself." That's exactly it. Our default is to protect self at all cost, to filter life through the question, "How does this affect me?" This is the essence of the safe life.

But the kingdom of heaven (also called the kingdom of God) is exactly the opposite. It flips the magnet around and pushes outward. It begins with the love of God, who meets all needs and fills all voids, and then it draws our attention out toward others. It leads us low instead of high. It flips the question of our lives from "How will this affect my life?" to "How will my life affect them?"

The kingdom of heaven ... flips the questions of our lives from "How will this affect my life?" to "How will my life affect them?"

Here's where it all gets tricky: it isn't safe. At all. Safe Christianity's goal is "don't mess up." Safe Christianity defines sin as "bad stuff." We tell people, "Don't do bad stuff." We tell our kids, "Don't do bad stuff." We make lists of bad things to not do, modern-day versions of "Don't smoke, don't chew, don't go with guys who do."

But the Bible defines sin in a radically different way. Yes, it's lawlessness (1 John 3:4). Yes, it's when we know we ought to do good but don't (James 4:17). But it's even broader than both of these: "Whatever is not from faith is sin" (Rom. 14:23 NASB).

Faith. Strangely enough, we can engage in religious activities without faith. Really. We can attend church, work in ministry, do good works, and live pretty fabulous churchy lives—without faith. As I sat back and evaluated my life with agonizing honesty, I realized that not much in my life actually required faith.

Our sole vocation in life is to please God. I knew that part. But then another pesky little verse kept peeking up off the pages of Scripture: "Without faith it is impossible to please God" (Heb. 11:6 NIV). Was my life actually characterized by faith? A safe life requires no faith.

The truth was, my life was mostly just a churchy version of the American dream. I just put Jesus masks on all my idols, and they looked pretty good!

The problem was, it wasn't the kingdom of God. It was the kingdom of safe, of self, of work-hard-to-not-mess-up. The kingdom of God and the American dream have nothing in common. The kingdom of God says, Lose your life to find it. Give away in order to receive. Be crucified with Christ in order to truly live. I could exposit these verses until I was blue in the face, but how in heaven's name were we supposed to live them?

How does one live the blank? Walk by faith. Live trusting. Ditch "safe."

As everything unraveled and I began to see my churchy life with new eyes, I was terrified. I had no idea what any of this meant. Would we sell our dream home? Would we give away all our belongings and move to Africa? Would we go live under a bridge? Would we leave our jobs? Would I have to quit teaching the Bible because I was such a pathetic hypocrite? Would everyone think we were crazy? Fear gripped my heart when I thought of how this separation from "normal" would impact my closest relationships. Would my friends think I was judging them? Would I ever be invited to parties again? I read once that John the Baptist would have made a terrible dinner guest. Would following Jesus into new territory make us terribly weird? I didn't want to be the person everyone avoided!

Going the way of the kingdom meant facing the reality of not knowing how it would all go down. And God didn't tell us. He just took us by the hand and led us, one tiny step at a time. He said, *Trust.*

So when, a week later, we sensed God tell us to sell our brand-new house and give away almost half our income, it was just a representative step of obedience in something much bigger: he wanted us to sell the farm, in every way. He'd given us a peek into his glorious, unseen kingdom of heaven—now it was our move.

Literally. Would we, with joy, "sell the farm" in order to gain that treasure-filled field? Ditch "safe" and start to live by faith? The "For Sale" sign was up the following weekend.

Jesus made it very clear: where our treasure is, our heart will be. Even though it was only wood and mortar, our house represented my heart. My heart so prone to my own kingdom, my comfort, my control, my approval, my success. To sell the farm, so to speak, and say yes to whatever God called us to do, without knowing how it would all work out, meant only one thing: we would actually have to trust and live the blank.

THE BLESSEDNESS OF POSSESSING NOTHING[1]

When I think of *letting* go, I picture empty hands. Paul spoke of life in the upside-down kingdom as "having nothing, yet possessing everything" (2 Cor. 6:10). We are constantly tempted to grab and grasp, gripping whatever we can get our grubby little hands on. Not just material possessions. Anything that becomes a requirement for our happiness weasels its way into the holy throne room of our heart where God alone should reign. A. W. Tozer writes, "The pronouns *my* and *mine* look innocent enough in print, but their constant and universal use is significant. . . . They are verbal symptoms of our deep disease."[2]

Anything that becomes a requirement for our happiness weasels its way into the holy throne room of our heart where God alone should reign.

Do you remember, from the story of the Velveteen Rabbit, how love becomes real? When it's rubbed up against real people, when its fur is worn and the stitches come loose a bit. Love becomes real when it slams into the reality of life, lived out with the one person right in front of us.

Faith is similar. Faith becomes real when it's lived out in life. When all other false security is rooted out—when nothing else is allowed on the throne of our hearts and our only requirement for happiness is him—that's when we place all our weight on God. It is easy to sing of faith in God; it is quite another to actually rest our full confidence daily on him. It's like sitting down on a stool and lifting our feet off the floor. If the stool falls, we fall. That's trust.

Our faith must be supremely practical. Faith cannot be developed in the mind; we must experience the act of trusting God in the dirty waters of daily life. It wasn't until Naaman walked down to the shores of the Jordan that his faith became real. When he acted, when he stuck a toe in and then fully immersed himself, dipping down deep and letting go—when the waters overwhelmed him completely—he was healed. There's no way to do this without getting wet. To walk by faith, we have to actually take steps!

Every hero of the faith did this, walking a path of complete, practical surrender. Perhaps the most famous is Abraham, who "believed God, and it was counted to him as righteousness" (Rom. 4:3; see also Gen. 15:6). How did his belief become real? First, he lived the blank. At the command of God he set out, "not knowing where he was going" (Heb. 11:8). He literally put one foot in front of the other, having no idea where he was headed. This is what it means to live the blank.

Then, in perhaps the greatest test of the reality of his faith, God called Abraham to sacrifice his son, his only son. If we really *look* at this story, and refuse a cursory glance, we will be appalled. The story is horrific. I cannot comprehend how disturbing it would be to hear the voice of God commanding me to kill my only child. This story is offensive.

And it is the most accurate portrayal of what every believer must face, the abnegation of all things, the surrendering of that which is most dear, the sacrifice of our dearest, truest love.

They don't put this story in children's Bibles. You'll never see this verse on a coffee mug: "Take your son, your only son Isaac, whom you love, and go . . . offer him there as a burnt offering on one of the mountains of which I shall tell you" (Gen. 22:2).

There are so many levels to this surrender. On a faith level, Isaac was God's promise in the first place. He wasn't Abraham's dream—God initiated the whole thing, promising that through Isaac all the nations of the world would be blessed. Abraham's righteousness was counted to him because he had believed this promise. And now God was killing that promise! How was Abraham to cling to the promise and yet surrender it?

After we put our house on the market in response to God's initiative, we trudged through a yearlong process of trying to sell, showing it ninety-two times and dropping the price more than $50,000. At around eleven months, we contemplated quitting. It was too exhausting, and we were facing a major financial loss. This seemed like the ultimate failure. God had given us a dream of blessing the nations, and we had believed him. We'd acted in faith.

But even the dreams God gives must die. Just because it's from him doesn't mean it's ours to keep. I found that I not only had to surrender the dream house but I also had to surrender the dream to sell the dream house. Ha! Even today, as I type these words, God has another adventure in the works, and I'm finding a whole new level of surrender. God will stop at nothing—he is relentless in his pursuit of our hearts and will jealously guard his throne therein. He knows our only joy and peace and life come in letting him be our all, in our clinging to nothing except him.

On another level, the level of the affections, we see how the wording in the Scripture passage emphasizes the nearness of Isaac to his father's heart. Abraham's son, his only son, whom he loved. All lofty spiritual promises aside, this was his kid! We cannot even fathom. I hope you have never experienced the sorrow of losing a child, but if you have, I'm sure you can identify with this dad's agony. God waited until exactly the right moment to require Abraham's absolute surrender. This wasn't a cerebral exercise of faith. Abraham didn't have to sacrifice the promise until it had a face, until he'd fallen in love with it.

———— ⚜ ————

Abraham didn't have to sacrifice the promise until it had a face, until he'd fallen in love with it.

God does this with us too. Even the dreams he gives us must be allowed to die, and he often waits until they're partially fulfilled, until they have a face, until we fall in love. Then he calls us to surrender them, because only then will our affections be exposed. Only then can he resecure his rightful place on the throne of our hearts.

And only then can he swoop in, mighty and glorious, and fulfill his purposes. Once the inward sacrifice was complete in Abraham's heart, God interrupted before the physical sacrifice took place. Abraham fully expected to lose Isaac, yet he trusted God. Hebrews tells us Abraham reasoned that God could raise Isaac from the dead if need be (11:19)! Abraham trusted God with his son and with the promise, and although he had surrendered everything, he became infinitely richer.

There is the treasure in the field. It is inward and eternal. It is the kingdom of God. It is what we gain when we lose. It's the glorious stuff that only faith can buy. It is what we discover when we venture into the unknown, into the blank.

FOR THE JOY

All of this has been rather heavy, yes? Sacrificing children, letting go of everything, possessing nothing. It can feel like adding heavy burdens, as if the sacred mundane is just a lifelong series of sacrifices, moping around as mommy martyrs.

The truth is, though, that all of this is actually the path to joy. As Jeff and I began intentionally turning our focus to the needy world around us, we began to feel a part of our hearts come alive. In a strange way, we felt like the man in Matthew 13:44: in his joy, he sold all he had for the treasure. No arm-twisting or guilt mongering going on here. He was thrilled to do this because he'd finally become aware of the true value hidden in the field. He finally saw the worth of what's unseen.

After we put our house on the market and made the plunge toward giving away a large percentage of our income, it was like someone turned on a rushing faucet of God's power and presence in my life. The day we put our house up for sale, I sat studying God's Word, weeping over his goodness and grace. Little stresses melted away in the big picture of blessing God's world.

When our house sold, we moved into a dumpy rental property. When we first saw the ad for it, I told Jeff, "That is the ugliest house I've ever seen." I had this romantic idea in my mind about what "living simply" would be. I hadn't anticipated exactly how ugly this simple living could be. And yet . . .

As the weeks went by, something strange happened: the ugly turned beautiful. When we moved in, I told Jeff, "I feel as if someone just took his hands off my throat. I feel like I can breathe for the first time." To my amazement, we found profound joy in that home. No more keeping up with the Joneses. No more comparing my house with anyone else's. (I could guarantee my house was uglier than everyone else's, so there was no need for comparison!) This one small step out of the rat race, of letting go of trying to keep up, brought more freedom and true joy than we'd ever experienced. I was no longer trying to please anybody else . . . but God.

This is freedom, friends. This is joy. It is for the joy that we willingly let go of all things. Of course, not everyone is called to sell their home. The journey will look different for each of us. But we're wise to hunt for that treasure and lay aside whatever we must to invest in the eternal kingdom of God. This isn't dreary, obligatory offering or begrudging giving; this is the delighted handing over of all that is ours for all that is God's. It was for the joy set before Jesus that he endured the cross. He didn't love what was happening; there is nothing lovely or romantic about being hanged, bloody, on a cross. He despised the shame. He did it for the surpassing joy that lay beyond the degradation and suffering.

Jesus perfectly lived out the upside-down kingdom principle of losing one's life to find it. It is this handing over of our lives that brings true happiness, joy, and life. The secret is in the letting go. Doing so brings freedom. As we release control, comfort, success, and approval, we trust God and live the blank.

We ditch "safe" and face fear head on.

FEAR

If idols are the saboteurs of love, then fear is the enemy of faith. Fear is and will be our enemy, always. Nothing keeps us from true transformation faster and more fully than fear. Idols keep us from loving, pride keeps us from hearing, and fear keeps us from trusting. Fear is the one thing that keeps us clinging to "safe," that keeps us from living the blank. Of course it is. We're scared to death of that blank. Why? Because it's so . . . blank. Right?

It's so unknown. It's pitch black, and we're groping in the dark, grasping frantically for some familiar handles, anything to cling to—other than God. Clinging only to him is terrifying. Why? Because he's so very unmanageable.

Idols keep us from loving, pride keeps us from hearing, and fear keeps us from trusting.

The thing about God that makes us crazy is that he refuses to be managed. He seldom gives us formulas or five-year plans. More often than not, he shines a faint light one step ahead. That's it.

Why does he do this to us? Because his greatest goal is that we would learn to trust him. It is our faith, more precious than gold, that he desires to cultivate in our lives (1 Peter 1:7). He knows that without faith we will be utterly lost. It is only as we learn to trust him that true joy and transformation can take place. He will build our faith and earn our trust at all cost.

The entire message of the Bible can be summed up in two words from God: *Trust me.* Every story, every verse, every passage: *Trust me.* Every word points to the trustworthiness of God and demands that we place our unwavering trust in who he is and what he says.

The entire message of the Bible can be summed up in two words from God: *Trust me.*

Every day the greatest temptation I will face is to not trust God. To lean instead on my own understanding. To give in to fear. To live safe. To erect idols and hang safety nets to keep me from that terrifying trust.

Sometimes it's little stuff. I fear failing or disappointing people. I fear making a royal mess of my kids. I fear others' opinions. Fear always taps gently on the door. But sometimes it kicks down the door and threatens to swallow us whole.

In Mark chapter 5, we're dropped down into a desperate scene. Jesus has just healed a demoniac, and the crowds are pressing in all around him as he stands by the sea. Jairus bursts through the crowd. He is a ruler in the synagogue, an esteemed religious leader. He has a lot going for him—but his little daughter is dying.

My little Heidi sits beside me as I type these words. I lean in and kiss her round cheek, close to her mouth so I can inhale her breath. There is nothing like the sweetness of a little daughter. And here we see Jairus collapsed at Jesus's feet in utter desperation, imploring him: "My little daughter is at the point of death."

Jesus turns immediately and goes with the man. Hallelujah! Jesus is coming! He is going to do exactly as Jairus has asked and save the day. They hurry along, no time to waste, Jairus's heart pounding. There is hope.

But then, an unexpected delay. A woman presses through the crowd and reaches out to touch Jesus's garment. She grasps, desperate. Twelve years of suffering makes her brash—she cares nothing for the crowds or how inappropriate her action might be. *Oh God, let me just touch his garment.* She does, and she is immediately healed. Boom. This is awesome. But the whole ordeal stops Jesus and causes a delay. We're told nothing about what Jairus is doing during all this. I know that when I'm delayed on my way out the door, I can go sideways real fast. Road construction, traffic, you name it—it all makes me crazy. I cannot even fathom the agony of this father as Jesus patiently attends to the woman at his feet. *Please, Jesus. Now! This lady has a little bleeding—big deal. My daughter is dying. Can we move on?*

Jesus speaks quietly to the woman: "Daughter, your faith has made you well. Go in peace." Jairus is listening. *Daughter? What about* my *daughter?* And just when Jairus is beside himself with waiting, the word comes from a messenger: "She's already dead."

No. No, no, no. Oh friends, if only we could understand how real this is. This daddy's greatest nightmare—and my own, and very likely yours—has just come true.

Then, as Jairus absorbs the words, their weight snuffing every flicker of hope, Jesus speaks straight into Jairus's soul: "Fear not, only believe." *Trust me, Jairus.*

I can only imagine this father's inward response. *Trust you? You, who are busy healing other people and letting my daughter die? Trust you?*

But by some miracle, Jairus does just that.

Jesus pushes the crowds aside and pulls Jairus close, leading him into the blank, into the unknown. When Jesus insists Jairus's daughter is only sleeping, the crowds laugh and lose the opportunity to see heaven touch earth. But Jairus stays and sees. He believes Jesus's words more than what his eyes see. He believes the supernatural power of God is greater than the natural power of death. And his reward is to see the supernatural. He sees truth. Jesus raises the girl from the dead, and I can only imagine the new four-word anthem of this family's life: fear not, only believe.

BUILD YOUR KINGDOM HERE

Do we want to see God's kingdom come and God's will be done on earth as it is in heaven? The circumstances will take a thousand different forms, but every opportunity requires trust. Every single day we have the chance to forsake fear and just believe. And when we do, when we look at the world through God's Word, as we listen to his voice in daily life, as we engage in the dailiness of life and embrace the one he has placed in our path, then we learn to trust God and actually live the blank, live in the can't-see-where-I'm-going place of faith. Faith pleases God.

Our family is now on a completely different adventure of faith that has challenged me in exactly the opposite way from before. God called us to surrender our dream home in order to live frugally. We whittled down our budget to less than half of what we were spending. We moved to a different city and planted a church with no idea how we'd make ends meet. We didn't know where the church would meet, where we'd live, or how it would all pan out. It was the blankest blank I'd ever seen.

But *God!* Over the years he has faithfully met our every need. He's provided finances, housing, friendships, and a building where our church family can gather. He's changed lives, raised up leaders, and blown us all away with his power and provision. And I've become quite happy with my neat and tidy little life and my tiny income. It is the most joyous, blessed, life-giving adventure I've ever known.

But somewhere over the years, I unknowingly became proud of my extreme frugality, taking it on as my identity, even equating frugality with godliness. So God in his wisdom has once again launched an all-out assault on my comfort zone and called me to walk on new waters of faith.

We are still in the same city and same church, with the same housemates, but we are trusting God to help us be faithful in stewarding more of his resources for the specific benefit of his people. It's a little like building an ark. It seems a bit absurd, and there's an abundance of opportunities for outside criticism. But Noah trusted God and did what looked loony in his day.

Every step of faith seems foolish to the world.

Lay hands on a sick person?

Give away your money?

Stick with your terrible spouse?

Give up your rights?

Turn the other cheek?

It is impossible to walk by faith and live safe. It is impossible to walk by faith and not risk. Faith is risk, always. But it's God-informed risk. It's risk calculated by the truth. We're not talking stupid risk, selfish risk, worldly risk. This isn't the stuff of casinos and scratch-its. This isn't living in isolation and refusing the sound wisdom of trusted counselors. That's foolishness.

Our risk must first be purified by the absolute surrender of our lives to God.

This is risk that resonates with the mission of God. The stuff of Noah (a boat?), of Abraham (where, exactly?), of Moses (say what to Pharaoh?), the disciples (feed five thousand with a boy's sack lunch?), and of countless others who have gone before us, taking risks we can't even imagine. All for the glory of God and the furthering of his kingdom. The Bible is full of risk. Are our lives?

Our risk must first be purified by the absolute surrender of our lives to God. We trade our paltry plans for his glorious ones and discover a sacred purpose that adds holy weight to our ordinary days.

Grocery trips become precious opportunities to pinch pennies and send saved money to fill hungry bellies around the world. Our homes become sanctuaries, sacred spaces where lost and hurting souls can come in and find safety, a refuge in the storm. Our normal nine-to-five jobs become mission fields, chances to build bridges, make connections, and become all things to all people in order to win some to Christ (see 1 Cor. 9:22). Our daily walks provide time for picking up trash, praying over neighborhoods and people at bus stops, turning eyes upward to our glorious God, and whispering worship all along the way. Our parenting becomes disciple making, recognizing the world-changing potential within each little soul we clothe, bathe, feed. Our suffering, even, becomes material for sacrifice as we learn to praise God in the midst of it.

This sacred mundane provides everything we need for knowing, loving, and serving our great God. This is how our life song sings. As we trust, walk by faith, and live the blank, may our mundane resound: *let* your kingdom come!

7

THANK: Find Fulfillment

The one who offers thanksgiving as his
sacrifice glorifies me.
—Psalm 50:23

As I TYPE THESE words we're going 75 mph through the desert, headed back to Oregon from Arizona. Remember that three-thousand-mile road trip my family takes each year? We're on it. We just celebrated Thanksgiving with extended family and are beginning our trek back home. We've covered a lot of ground. Much of it is a blur, quite literally, as we fly along the freeway, sagebrush and cacti zooming past on the periphery. We've made this trip enough times, though, to be familiar with the terrain. The route we take is always the same, and we always return to the same place. What's different each time is us.

Each year, Jeff and I remark how different the kids are from the last time. Let me tell you, road trips are a lot easier with seven- and nine-year-olds than they are with a newborn and a two-year-old! This time around the kids can read, create, draw, and remember road marks. They can eat sandwiches in their seats and hold their bladders for a reasonable length of time between pit stops (hooray!). One of my favorite parts of this road-trip tradition is seeing the change in them, and in Jeff and me, from year to year.

We've covered a lot of ground together in this book as well, and now we're returning to where we began: worship. Our heart's home, if you will, is worship. Way back in the beginning, we discovered that our lives, our whole lives, were meant to be offered up as a living sacrifice (Rom. 12:1), not of atonement (Jesus did that!) but of continual praise (Heb. 13:15). This whole-life praise song rises to heaven and blesses God's heart as we embrace every ordinary moment as a means of worshipping him.

As we return to worship and our time together winds down, it is my hope and prayer that you are different as well. Just as my children change each year as we trek to Arizona, I pray that you are beginning to see some slightly perceptible differences in the sentence of your life. Sometimes the changes start small. Our kids are only an inch or two taller than last year. They are watching many of the same movies, eating the same snacks, whining during the same long stretches. Sometimes, though, the changes are significant. When we went from diapers to no diapers, for example, my happiness quotient soared.

The danger, however, is that we will move forward in some measure—traveling to new places, achieving some level of success or satisfaction, enjoying the thrill of victory—without returning to our heart's true home: worship. If we don't come back to thank God, the best work is aborted, the miracle is incomplete, and we miss the glory of true transformation.

Consider the ten lepers from Luke 17. They came to Jesus. They asked for mercy. Jesus came through and miraculously healed them by sending them to see the priests. They all went, obeying him by faith, and were healed physically of their disease. Then, remember what happened?

Only one came back to thank the Lord. That one, a Samaritan, "turned back, praising God with a loud voice; and he fell on his face at Jesus' feet, giving him thanks" (Luke 17:15–16). "Your faith has made you well," Jesus said, identifying this man as truly characterized by faith. This was the one who was wholly healed, mind, body, and spirit. This was the one who was *saved*. We can experience a lot of growth and success and change, but if we do not return to *thank*, we haven't truly been transformed from the inside out.

Let's not get this far, dear friends, only to quit before the work is complete. Let's not wander off like the lepers, forgetting to return to worship the King. Let's not be content for surface change, no matter how good it looks from the outside. Let's go all the way and let him save us through and through.

We know our lives are a living sacrifice, and God tells us specifically the kind of sacrifice that pleases him, that glorifies him, that makes him smile: "The one who offers thanksgiving as his sacrifice glorifies me" (Ps. 50:23).

The consummation of the sacred mundane: *thanks*.

Remember that the word *sacrifice* comes from the Hebrew *korban*, which means to "come close." What is the sacrifice that pleases God, the "sacred doing" that brings us close to him?

Thanks.

If we haven't grown in thanks, we haven't grown.

Thanks is the secret that makes this whole thing soar. Without true thanksgiving, all these LET steps are just gimmicky behavior modifications. We might reach a dozen lofty goals, but without thanksgiving, we're still not pleasing God. And, I would say, we aren't pleased either. If the Creator created us to worship him through thanksgiving, then we will never find true fulfillment until we're functioning as intended. God is so glorious and wise that he created us to be fully alive, satisfied, fulfilled, completed when we are doing what pleases him—giving thanks. Humble thanks is the consummation of a sacred, Godward life. Thanks is the natural outworking of a transformed heart.

If we haven't grown in thanks, we haven't grown.

Now, take heart. I write to you as a fellow failing thanker. I was tempted to simply type, "Read Ann Voskamp's *One Thousand Gifts*" as the text of this chapter. Ann is the resident expert on thanksgiving, not me; I don't even know where my half-finished gift list is. But while I wholeheartedly

recommend her book as the go-to text on growing in thanksgiving, I
thought there might be a few other failing thankers out there besides me,
and we could band together and learn something too.

The truth is, we know we want to be thankful. We know it's the secret
to glorifying God and finding fulfillment for our restless hearts. So, if
gratitude is our goal, then what has gone wrong? I hope to offer a fresh
perspective on what keeps us from glorifying God through thanksgiving.
Let's begin by dealing honestly with our disappointments.

THE GOD WHO DISAPPOINTS

As I type these words, it is the day after Thanksgiving. This day now has
its own name and is celebrated in its own right. It is Black Friday.

There's nothing wrong with great deals. I like them too. But this surge
of sales-frenzied consumers that floods the stores each year certainly tells
us something about ourselves: we want more stuff. Why is it that on the
heels of a holiday that explicitly celebrates being full and grateful and satisfied, that we can scarcely get the dishes done before scampering out the
door for a sale on more stuff?

I'm not throwing stones. I feel the pull too. This past week I have struggled to be grateful. Even though we were surrounded by loving people,
with plenty of food and sunshine and even leisure time, something kept
snagging my spirit. Instead of rising up in unobstructed thanks, my heart
kept dipping low in discouragement. Why?

Disappointment. Chances are there is an unidentified, beneath-the-
surface disappointment that's silently stunting our spiritual growth, like a
lid slammed down on our offering of praise.

When I speak of disappointment, I'm referring to the mundane suffering that's part of our ordinary, daily experience. Mini sufferings. While
we may be hesitant to categorize these inconveniences and frustrations as
genuine "suffering," I think we could all agree that the word *disappointment* does fit the bill. Ongoing disappointment wears us down to the core.
Like a slow leak, daily disappointment drains our thankfulness, leaving
us empty rather than full.

Disappointment can apply to a wide variety of discouraging circumstances. I recently had a conversation with a friend who is being sued for $3 million. He said, in his humble, soft-spoken manner, that the situation was "disappointing." I'd say! I could use the same word to describe how I feel when bumper-to-bumper Los Angeles traffic delays our much-anticipated arrival by several hours. Traffic is disappointing. Lawsuits are disappointing. The essence of both is the same: thwarted expectation.

The dictionary defines "disappointment" as exactly that: thwarted expectation. Quite simply, disappointment happens when circumstances are other than what we expected, and not in a good way. It all comes back to expectation.

What does this have to do with thanks? When we are in a cycle of disappointment—and it is a cycle—our thanks is grounded. And while our mundane sufferings do work for us in some ways, they also have the potential to hinder our thanks.

---

*When we are in a cycle of disappointment—
and it is a cycle—our thanks is grounded.*

So, does disappointment crush us or make us stronger? Which is it?

It depends on how we deal with disappointment. There are two distinct paths we can follow that lead us to two distinct cycles. And I believe God strategically disappoints us so we will learn to follow a particular path into glorious fulfillment, transformation, faith, joy, worship.

Yes, God disappoints us.

Disappointment is simply the outcome of thwarted expectations, but I believe it is God himself who does the thwarting. A quick survey of Scripture will confirm this.

Abraham

God promises Abraham he will be the father of nations. It was God's idea, remember? Then what happened? Abraham can't have kids. He's disappointed. For *twenty-five* years his expectation is thwarted. The long, gnawing ache of disappointment becomes his constant companion. If you've ever struggled with infertility, you know this pain. Every single month—hopes up, hopes dashed. This would've added up to *three hundred months* of disappointment.

Joseph

God gives Joseph a dream revealing that he will be a ruler and his brothers will bow down to him. Meanwhile, Joseph winds up dumped in a pit and left for dead, then sold as a slave, following which he's wrongly accused of attempted rape, thrown into prison, and forgotten for two more years. I'd say that's disappointing.

Moses

God gives Moses a burning desire to deliver his people. But Moses messes things up and ends up fleeing for his life and tending sheep in the desert for forty years. Then, when Moses is sent at last to deliver Israel, the glorious exodus he thought would lead straight into the Promised Land degrades into forty years of leading a grumbling multitude around in circles in the wilderness. Talk about a letdown!

David

David is anointed king of Israel by Samuel, and the Spirit of the Lord comes upon him. Then what? Does he step into his reign immediately? Far from it! Saul tries to kill him over and over, and David spends ten to fourteen *years* fleeing in the desert, living in caves and running for his life. Instead of reigning as king, he is a homeless man on the run. Not exactly what he expected.

The Disciples

God promised to send a Messiah who would come to deliver his people and save the world. The disciples expect a powerful political leader. Then comes Jesus, who neither fights nor takes over anything, but who is a lowly servant and calls them to be lowly servants, willingly losing their lives. Then Jesus does the unthinkable: goes and gets himself killed without even putting up a fight.

His disciples have left everything—jobs, families, possessions, status—to follow this man who claims he is a king and will be the deliverer of Israel. And now their Savior is dead. It's all over. No revolution. No overthrowing the Roman government. It was all for naught. This, friends, is the last word in thwarted expectations.

You Bible-reading folks know that there is a better ending to all these stories. We have the benefit of reading the stories after the fact. But put yourself smack-dab in the middle and you can feel the sting of disappointment these godly men felt.

Even the godliest characters in Scripture experienced profound disappointment, and it was part of their sacred journey.

I share these stories because we must understand that godly people experience disappointment. I've often said to myself, "I shouldn't feel this way." How helpful is that? Even the godliest characters in Scripture experienced profound disappointment, and it was part of their sacred journey. To say, "You shouldn't have expectations" isn't helpful either. Telling ourselves not to have expectations, or attempting a sort of numb indifference toward life, won't bring transformation and thanksgiving. There's nothing godly about worst-case-scenario thinking. Instead, understanding that God *purposefully* disappoints us will help us let these minor trials work worship into our lives. But first we have to understand the process.

THE GOD WHO GRIEVES

The clearest example of God's intentional disappointment is in John 11. You are likely familiar with the story. Our main characters are Jesus and his dear friends Lazarus, Mary, and Martha. We read in verse 1 that Lazarus is ill. We also are reminded in verse 2 that this is the same Mary who anointed Jesus with costly ointment and wiped his feet with her hair.

Jesus dearly loves this man and his two sisters. In fact, when the sisters send for Jesus, they say, "The one you love is sick" (v. 3 NIV).

Let's begin with a basic question: Why do they call for Jesus? They expect him to heal Lazarus. Pretty logical reasoning.

Lazarus is sick.

Jesus loves Lazarus.

Jesus heals.

Therefore, call for Jesus to come heal Lazarus.

Sounds reasonable. I have a problem. Jesus loves me. Jesus fixes problems. Therefore, I should tell Jesus my problem so he can fix it.

Jesus's response is one of the most important statements in Scripture: "This illness does not lead to death. It is for the glory of God, so that the Son of God may be glorified" (v. 4). God will be glorified; it's actually safe to say that all he does (or doesn't do) is for this overarching purpose. We don't know whether Mary and Martha receive this message back, but either way, they expect Jesus to heal Lazarus.

What does Jesus do? Thwarts their expectations.

Read verses 5 and 6 and I think you'll agree they're utterly counterintuitive. Jesus loves Mary and Martha and Lazarus, so what does he do? He stays put for two more days. *Because* he loves them. This is so significant. It means *Jesus deliberately let Lazarus die.*

Jesus deliberately let Lazarus die.

Remember, God doesn't just passively use disappointment for good. He disappoints us on purpose. Everything God does is deliberate. Jesus deliberately waits two more days so that Lazarus will die. To confirm Jesus's intention, in verses 14–15 we read these words of his to his disciples: "Lazarus has died, and for your sake I am glad that I was not there, so that you may believe. But let us go to him."

Say what? Jesus is glad Lazarus has died? This seems heartless—until we look deeper. Jesus is willing to kill one expectation in order to birth another that is far more glorious. That is why he's glad—he knows the outcome. Mary and Martha's shattered hopes are about to become their doorway to a breathtaking revelation of Jesus's true identity as the resurrection and the life. The truth is, God is so much greater than we even realize.

God wants to build our faith in him. He wants us to trust, to believe the unseen more than what we see, to live the blank and believe him no matter what our senses are screaming at us. God wants the supernatural reality to be more real to us than our physical reality. And he will do whatever it takes to accomplish that.

God wants the supernatural reality to be more real to us than our physical reality.

But it doesn't seem logical that God would build our belief by disappointing us, right? If he wants to help us believe, it seems like he should immediately fulfill our every wish so we'd know he is able. Instead, he does the exact opposite. Remember Romans 5:1–5 where we learned the process of *hupomone* working its way into our lives? Let's look again: suffering (disappointment) ➺ *hupomone* (endurance) ➺ character (transformation) ➺ hope.

True hope in God grows in the gnarly garden of thwarted expectations.

When Jesus finally shows up late to the party, Lazarus is dead. Way dead. Jesus doesn't just miss the boat by a few minutes but by *four days*. He really blew it! Sure, Jesus has raised some people from the dead before, but their deaths were fresh while Lazarus is already buried. Gone. All hope is gone.

This is the remarkable thing about God. He doesn't just kind of disappoint us. He way disappoints us. It isn't like Lazarus has just breathed his last, and maybe there's hope of reviving him within the hour. When God lets something die in our lives, he lets it die all the way. Dead and buried four days. He lets it sink in. He lets us grieve, wail, weep. When God disappoints us, he chooses the things that will cut to the very core of our being. It sometimes seems savage, cruel even, but it's the quickest route to the total transformation of our souls.

Picture this with me: Mary and Martha have placed all their hope in Jesus to save their beloved brother, and Jesus has utterly and completely failed them. They are devastated. Have you ever felt that way—devastated because God didn't show up like you hoped?

Can I just step aside from the Scriptures and look you in the eye for a moment? We have all had those times when God allowed our very dearest—a person, a hope, a plan, a love, a dream—to die. We might be hesitant to admit it. We might be afraid of offending God or not sounding spiritual enough. I plead with you to deal honestly with God. How has he disappointed you? How have his ways sometimes seemed savage? How has his deliberate disappointment felt calculated or cruel? The most significant disappointment of my life, to date, felt so carefully crafted that I cried out to God, "You tricked me!" Fifteen years later, I can see that indeed it was carefully crafted, with relentless love, for my eternal good. I am grateful, but at the time, I could barely breathe I was so caught off guard by his apparent cruelty.

We might be afraid of offending God or not sounding spiritual enough. I plead with you to deal honestly with God.

Mary and Martha's disappointment isn't even thinly veiled. They make it clear, and I love them for it. Martha runs to Jesus, and the first words out of her mouth are filled with bitter disappointment: "Lord, if you had been here, my brother would not have died" (John 11:21).

Translation: (Ahem) Jesus. If you had done something, this wouldn't have happened!

We've thought this too, yes? Thankfully, Martha still believes. And what happens next will likely be the most miraculous encounter of her life.

Jesus goes to the tomb, and *enters into* their disappointment with them. This part amazes me. Jesus knew he was going to raise Lazarus, but he still chose to enter into the pain and grief and suffering of these precious people. The shortest verse in the Bible, John 11:35, is "Jesus wept." He was "deeply moved in his spirit and greatly troubled" (v. 33). He felt their pain.

The greatest danger we face in our disappointment is believing the lie that God is somehow aloof—that he watches from a distance, perhaps slightly amused at our pathetic whimpering as we slog through the suffering of life. But this is not the God we serve. The God we serve and love and worship is a compassionate Father who chooses to experience with us every ounce of the pain we endure. When he chooses to afflict us, he afflicts himself. If you are hurting, dear friend, God is hurting with you. He bore, and he bears, our sorrows.

God weeps with you. He may be the God who disappoints, but he is also the God who grieves. Because of this, we can bravely and honestly enter in to our disappointments, knowing that God is there too.

The truth we see from this extreme example of suffering also applies to the everyday, mini sufferings of life. In fact, it is precisely in these smaller disappointments where we learn to interact with God in a healthy way and allow him to birth true hope in our hearts. These smaller things, perhaps, seem petty compared with death and disease, but they have just as much potential for hijacking our gratitude and grounding our praise. Too often we think that thanksgiving comes by ignoring these small things. It doesn't. True thanks comes by entering in to them honestly and discovering God is there. Finding him is what fuels our authentic thanksgiving.

THE PAINT IS NOT "PEAR"

Think your struggle with daily disappointment is too insignificant to lay before God? Let me share an example from my own life that I doubt you can beat for shallowness.

When Jeff and I left California and moved back to Oregon, we bought a house in eager anticipation of our first child. It was a great deal, and I liked almost everything about it—except the paint. Every wall was awful.

I'm not one to shy away from DIY, so I quickly picked out paint colors and, since I was pregnant, set Jeff to work. The only challenge was the master bedroom. It was large, with a tall, vaulted ceiling. Upon seeing that soaring ceiling and quickly estimating the cost and effort required to repaint it, I quickly insisted that I liked the color.

There. Done. I like the color. Yes. It's . . . it's . . . *pear.*

The only problem was, it wasn't pear. It was a horrendous green that wasn't lime or apple or avocado or pistachio, and certainly not pear. There was no delicious food this color! It was just ugly.

But I had decided: it was pear.

Now, nothing is wrong with telling yourself to stop being picky and make do with what you have. The problem was, I did that with a disturbingly large portion of my life. Plaster on a smile, raise the eyebrows, and speak with exclamation points: "I like it! I like it! I like it!" This approach just doesn't work. No amount of positive thinking could change the fact that the paint was *not* pear.

Again, please understand: the point is not to have perfect circumstances. Having all our expectations met won't work thankfulness into us because disappointments aren't the problem. Failing to honestly acknowledge our disappointments is the problem. We hide how we feel. Why? Out of fear. We're afraid that by admitting something hurts, bothers, or disappoints us, we'll be seen as weak, shallow, unspiritual, or needy. By others, by ourselves, by God. So we pretend, and often we don't even know we're doing it.

> We're afraid that by admitting something hurts, bothers, or disappoints us, we'll be seen as weak, shallow, unspiritual, or needy.

In his fabulous book *Inside Out,* Dr. Larry Crabb points out that in order to stay happy, sane, and content, most of us pretend that disappointments do not exist. We do this not because we're super-spiritual but because we're self-protective. Rather than open ourselves to the possible negative consequences of sharing what we really think and feel, we slap on a spiritual smile and say, loud and proud, "The paint is pear!"

I read Crabb's book in the midst of my own self-delusion, and scales seemed to fall from my eyes. That was it! Jeff must have thought I'd gone stark raving mad when he returned from work that day and I ran to the door joyfully shouting, "Guess what? I hate that green paint! It *isn't* pear. It's horrendous and I hate it. Woo hoo!"

When met with this strange enthusiasm, I'm sure Jeff thought, "Great, I'll have to paint that stupid room!" But no, I assured him: "You don't have to paint the room because I don't have to have perfectly painted walls in order to be happy. I can hate the color on my walls and still rejoice and give thanks and be perfectly content."

The key is this: if we think we have to lie to ourselves and others by pretending we are okay with everything in our lives, we will never become profoundly content. Our flimsy facade of seeming contentment will be nothing more than a self-protective cover for our inwardly unhappy lives. True thanksgiving flows from an authentically satisfied heart.

We must begin with baby steps, being honest with ourselves and God: this is different from what I expected. This hurts. I don't like the paint. Lord, can you help me be both honest and rejoicing?

God can work wonders with an honest heart. Where do you need to honestly admit that, really, the paint isn't pear?

THANK YOU FOR YOU

My silly paint story is a lighthearted example of the disappointments we inevitably face. Some are more significant and painful. Just last week I found myself with a nagging tinge of disappointment, but I successfully ignored it for four or five days. It had to do with a relationship, and I knew it was stupid. I tried to conceive of my disappointment any other way than what it was—ridiculous. No matter how I tried to spin it in my head, it didn't sound legit. But I still felt it. Keenly. And it wasn't getting better, because I hadn't engaged with God in the midst of it.

Remember how we have to mesh gears for movement to happen? We likewise have to engage with God in the realness of life—in the petty disappointments, hurt feelings, and upset expectations. Only then can he move us. Only then can he change us.

When I finally did sit down with God and got dead-bang honest, pouring out my disappointment in prayer in ridiculously honest words that spilled straight out of my silly, shallow heart, guess what happened: he turned my heart around.

Truly. I saw the matter clearly. And more importantly, I saw him. I found God in the midst of my disappointment and realized he felt my pain too. He knew that even though it sounded silly, it was still legit. He was the only one who could really understand—and he did. He came in, comforted me, and moved me out of my self-focus, not by pandering to my pity party but by leading me through it to thanksgiving.

God taught me to thank him in the midst of my disappointment because *he* was in the midst of it. All thanksgiving is really just some variation of *God, thank you for you!*

A habit of thanks is simply a habit of meeting him in the midst.

EXPECTANCY WITHOUT EXPECTATION

Let's go back for a moment to the definition of disappointment: thwarted expectations. It all comes back to expectations. As we saw with our biblical examples, our expectations are often good. Abraham, Joseph, Moses, David, Mary, Martha, the disciples—all these godly people had godly expectations. Right?

Sort of.

There is a subtle difference between living in *expectancy* and living with *expectations*. And while it may seem to be splitting hairs at first, the difference is vast and significant when carried along its natural progression. In fact, I believe expectation leads us into the vicious cycle of disappointment, while expectancy leads us into the glorious cycle of fulfillment.

Expectation is fueled by fear; expectancy is fueled by faith.

Expectation leads to disappointment; expectancy leads to fulfillment.

The two cycles look like this:

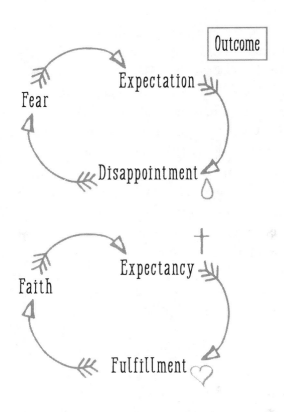

Whenever we are faced with a need, desire, or some unknown, we all know we are supposed to choose faith, even though we're usually facing an onslaught of fear. When we look to the future, we can't see a thing. Up ahead looks blank—and that's terrifying. So, in order to feel better about things, we paint a picture of what we want to happen, and we hold it up in front of our faces, and stare at it. We desperately need something to look forward to, even if we make it up ourselves. Looking directly into the dark unknown is way too scary, so we stare at the fabricated picture of what we hope will happen. We say we're trusting in God, hoping in God, waiting on God, but we're really trusting in our picture, hoping for our picture, waiting for our picture.

That picture is an *expectation*. Now, God loves us too much to let this all work out. He knows that the only way we will truly trust him and know him is if our expectation is shattered, forcing us to look through that fabricated, flimsy picture straight into the face of God.

The trick is, it takes faith to see what is unseen. It takes actual faith to look at a God whom our minds cannot fully conceive. It takes faith to stare into the darkness, the blank, the unknown, and see him there.

This faith vision is called *expectancy*. It means that instead of staring at my picture of what I want to happen, I stare at the beauty and character of God. I stare at who he is. I choose to see him rather than a picture I put together in my mind. I live in holy anticipation because my gaze is fixed on the glorious face of the God who is good and does good. This expectancy is fueled by informed faith. I know my God.

> Instead of staring at my picture of what I want to happen,
> I stare at the beauty and character of God.

But if I'm living in fear-inspired expectation, God will gladly disappoint me in order to shatter my expectation picture and birth true, faith-filled expectancy in my heart.

The problem is, this whole process is cyclical. When we choose not to acknowledge the sting of disappointment or enter into it, thus discovering in its midst God's tender presence and fixing our eyes on his face, then we inevitably choose instead to ignore it, and we further anesthetize ourselves by setting up a picture. An expectation. Inevitably that expectation too gets shattered—but again, rather than enter into the disappointment, we choose still another picture. It's a vicious cycle, and often we live caught up in it.

Fear ➤→ *Expectation* ➤→ *Disappointment*
Around and around we go.

But what if, instead, we refused to paint a picture of expectation? Instead of being driven by fear, we can choose true faith, which says, *I have no idea how this is going to look, but I know what he looks like. I know his character. I know his love. I know that what his Word says is true. I know his timing is perfect and his ways are perfect. I know he is good and does good. And while I will always pray specifically and purposefully for what I know to be his will, I will also leave the details to him. I will not overly concern myself with the ins and outs of his ways. He's already told me they are beyond my searching and scrutiny (Rom. 11:33). It's his world, his plan, his purpose. I don't have to have a certain outcome, because I have the certain One.*

This pleases the heart of God—this faith. It puts him above any prayer request or heartfelt desire. This is how we trust and live the blank, fixing our spiritual eyes on the unseen beauty and goodness of God.

And you know what? This kind of faith brings results. We can't control it or control him, but this true faith and expectancy brings fulfillment.

Faith ➤→ Expectancy ➤→ Fulfillment

While God purposefully disappoints us, he is ultimately the God of fulfillment. He is a covenant God who always keeps his promises. He delights in swooping in and saving the day. He loves answering prayer and providing for his people. But he will always do it his way, on his terms, for his glory. Psalm 66:10–12 outlines the entire process like this:

> For you, O God, have tested us;
>   you have tried us as silver is tried.
> You brought us into the net;
>   you laid a crushing burden on our backs;
> you let men ride over our heads;
>   we went through fire and through water;
> yet you have brought us out to a place of abundance.

Those stories I shared about God's disappointing different people in the Bible—we never completed them, did we? They end with glorious fulfillment.

Abraham's wife, Sarah, does bear children, and his descendants outnumber the stars in the sky.

Joseph does come to power in Egypt and use his influence to save the lives of millions.

Moses does lead his people to the Promised Land.

David does become king, the greatest king who ever lived.

Mary and Martha do see their brother healed, miraculously raised from the dead.

The disciples do see Jesus conquer sin and death, and we are still watching the glorious fulfillment of Jesus's establishing his eternal kingdom over all.

Fulfillment does come—but only after God shatters the expectations of his people and births true expectancy in their hearts instead.

How do we know the difference? How can we tell if we are truly living in holy expectancy or whether we are simply setting up expectations? Let's look together at a few key distinctions.

EXPECTANCY

For and With

Expectancy is not only believing God *for* something but also trusting God *with* something. *For* implies that we are believing God to do a specific thing. If this specific thing is in line with his will, awesome! To know the will of the Father, we can look to Jesus, because Jesus always did what pleased the Father. We can confidently believe God for the things we see Jesus doing.

But we must also trust God *with* the situation. *With* implies that we are handing over the thing (hope, relationship, dream, etc.) and allowing God to work in his own good, miraculous way. It is the essence of saying, "You are God and you are good. I trust you will orchestrate this in a way that is for your glory and for my good." In a situation where God's promise is clear, Abraham is a perfect example. He handed over his son while still believing God would be faithful to his promise. Abraham believed *for* and trusted *with*.

Shadrach, Meshach, and Abednego are a perfect example of when a specific promise *isn't* clear. God promises to protect us, but he also promises that his followers will suffer persecution and possibly martyrdom. When these men were thrown into the fiery furnace, they trusted God with their circumstances: "Our God whom we serve is able to deliver us . . . out of your hand, O king. But if not, be it known to you, O king, that we will not serve your gods" (Dan. 3:17–18). They are saying, "We not only trust God *for* deliverance out of this trial, but we also trust God *with* this trial, and he can do whatever he pleases."

True Hope, Not "Getting Hopes Up"

Expectancy is what births true hope in our hearts. Sadly, we've watered down this word *hope* with the phrase "Getting our hopes up." We say we're trying not to "get our hopes up" because the result will be disappointment—right? Most often we use the word *hope* pessimistically: hope = disappointment.

But nothing could be further from the true meaning of hope. Romans 5:5 (where we looked at *hupomone* and how hope is born) clearly states that "hope does not disappoint" (NASB).

That's the hope the psalmist spoke of in Psalm 42: "Why are you cast down, O my soul . . . hope in God" (vv. 5, 11). Hope is in the person and promise of God. No matter what setbacks or circumstances slam us in the face, faith-filled expectancy keeps us anchored in the hope of God—that God is trustworthy, has our best in mind, and will show up. Hope—the Bible kind of hope—does not disappoint. Let's forever banish "getting hopes up" from our vocabulary and call it what it is: "getting expectations up." Let's sanctify hope once again.

Wait on the Lord, Not People

The day I drove with my friend Dawson up I-5 north to Portland, I was neck-deep in a painful romantic relationship with a boy I'll call Jason. We were in an awkward state of limbo, and I was unsure whether we were going to split up or stay together. My good friend asked me how I was doing. I responded, "Oh fine. Just waiting on the Lord."

He looked over at me and gently asked, "Are you waiting on the Lord or waiting on Jason?"

Did you know that a "gentle tongue can break a bone" (Prov. 25:15 NIV)? You bet it can! In that instant, my expectation shattered. I knew he was right. In all my "holy waiting," I was really just wallowing in my own disappointments and waiting for this man to make up his mind about my future. Suddenly I knew the truth: I wasn't waiting on the Lord at all; I was waiting on a man.

Waiting on God is not always clear-cut because sometimes it does include waiting on some concrete things such as job applications and relationships. But the key is this: waiting on God keeps our eyes firmly fixed on him, whereas waiting on a person or circumstance focuses on things that change and shift, twist and turn, leading to disappointment and anxiety. It's waiting for the world to change to fit the picture we're holding up in order to shield us from the blankness in front of us.

Waiting on God keeps our eyes firmly fixed on him, whereas waiting on a person or circumstance focuses on things that change and shift.

Psalm 62:5 says it like this: "My soul, wait silently for God alone, for my expectation is from Him" (NKJV; of course I'd insert "expectancy" instead of "expectation"). We wait only for him. We fix our eyes on him. No matter how circumstances and people change with the weather, he remains the same. We wait for him.

Now, I don't mean to convey that waiting on God versus our own expectations is a simple delineation and the difference is always crystal clear. It's not. It's a battle. A fight for faith over fear. We won't get it right all the time. It's not about merely not messing up. When we find ourselves facing disappointment, we can enter into it honestly, knowing God will meet us in its midst; and we can ask him to reveal any flimsy picture expectation we have fabricated out of fear. We can turn from that expectation and choose to trust instead, looking into the blank and living in expectancy. We aren't only trusting God *for*; we're also trusting God *with*. We aren't "getting our hopes up"; we're anchored in the hope that never disappoints. We aren't waiting on people or circumstances; we're waiting on God alone.

Our eyes are fixed on him.

THE OFF-/ON-RAMP OF THANKS

Let's consider the two cycles again.

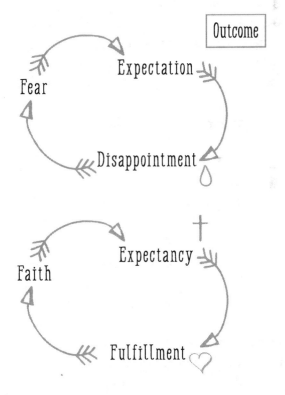

We've seen how they carry us around and around. The real question we must address is, how do we get from one cycle to the other?

On a road trip, the key to getting to your destination is finding the correct ramp that takes you off one road and onto another. Once you've navigated the ramp, you're set. The freeway, or whatever road you're on, will take you where you need to go.

As with the highway ramps, there are ramps for these cycles. Thanks is the ramp that leads to the fulfillment cycle, and lack of thanks leads to the disappointment cycle. Our heart's home is worship, praise, and thanksgiving, and a holy habit of returning to thanks will keep us living in faith-filled expectancy.

We must always return to thanks. It is the quickest off-ramp from the cycle of disappointment, and it sets us on the stable road of faith and expectancy. Choosing to thank God, even in the midst of disappointment, directs us off our fearful route and lands us smack-dab in the middle of God's glorious presence.

Thanks is where we finally find ourselves doing what we were created to do.

Thanks is where we finally find fulfillment.

Our life goal is fulfilling God's plans for our lives—and in doing so, we ourselves experience fulfillment.

See, fulfillment isn't merely a self-focused, superficial goal. Fulfillment, in the godly sense, is glorious and good! God created us for fulfillment. He desires to fulfill his purpose on earth in and through us. He wants to fulfill the dreams that *he* puts in our hearts. He wants to fulfill his plans. In prayer, we listen to God so we can discern his voice sharing with us his will, his plan, his purposes; then we partner with him in carrying out his will. Our life goal is fulfilling God's plans for our lives—and in doing so, we ourselves experience fulfillment.

We are most satisfied when we are satisfied in God. When his plans are our plans; his goals, our goals. When we find our hope and joy and purpose within his good will, we find ourselves gloriously fulfilled.

Remember our friend Naaman? God purposefully disappointed his expectations because God wanted to fulfill a far greater purpose. He wanted to heal not only Naaman's leprosy but also his heart. God wanted to free Naaman from more than just leprosy—he also wanted to free Naaman from himself.

Naaman brought his lofty expectations and a chariot loaded with his own worth and resources. Only when Naaman let go of everything and entered in to the disappointment, dipping down deep into those dirty waters, did he truly discover the God of Israel. God knew that Naaman needed something far greater than physical healing; he needed God. After the glorious transformation, Naaman announces, "From now on [I] will not offer burnt offering or sacrifice to any god but the Lord" (2 Kings 5:17).

As we dip down deep into our own daily disappointments, abandoning our expectations and personal resources and honestly acknowledging our weaknesses and pain, we discover that God delights to meet us in the midst. He weeps with us. He willingly disappoints us so that we'll leave it all behind and dip into those waters. He knows that then we can live in the vividness of his real world, not the scratchings of our frantically painted pictures. He knows that then we will find salvation, turn from false gods, be made whole. He knows that then our heart's cry will ever and always be some variation of "God, thank you for you!"

8

LET Your Life Be Poured Out

❖━━━━◆━━━━❖

Take my love, my Lord, I pour
at Thy feet its treasure store.
Take myself and I will be
ever only all for Thee.
—Frances R. Havergal, 1874

WE'RE AT THE END, friends. It's bittersweet to see our time together come to a close. It has been such a good journey. I've changed so much through the writing of these words; I pray you've changed a bit through the reading. Please know: this isn't a professional endeavor for me. I've poured my heart into your hands right here. By the time you hold this book, it'll be nearly two decades that sacred mundane has been the love of my life— longer than my children, longer than my marriage.

When I first typed the introduction to this book, my daughter had just turned two. She'll be eight when these words are finally in print. This journey of writing has taken more turns than I can count, and the road has been much longer than I planned.

And it has been perfect.

This journey has stripped me of pride and ambition and led me down low into love. I have prayed for you, reader. I have prayed that God would take this tiny offering, my heart poured out on paper, and use it to somehow bless your life. As we close, I would like to leave you with the last drop of my outpoured heart: a plea to let your own life be poured out.

As the apostle Paul neared the end, he described his life as a poured-out drink offering (2 Tim. 4:6). In our culture, we often picture our lives as a long journey of filling. We seek to gain, accumulate, achieve. We want to fill our homes, fill our résumés, fill our bank accounts, fill our stomachs, fill our schedules, fill our own sense of achievement. But as Paul neared death and reflected on all his days, he saw it as one long opportunity to pour. To empty. So, as we close our time together, I'd like to reflect on this image of a life poured out.

<hr>

Am I willing to let my life be poured out?

When we began I asked you to consider the sentence of your life. There was a *but* and it was a problem, yes? I have talked with thousands of women through my years of speaking, and we all share this: we want to change. We want to flourish. No one wants to live stuck, impotent, weak, failing, unhealthy. Many are eager to embrace the truths that are taught—turning from sin, confessing the untruths we believe about God, letting go of control. But in this whole process, the real crux that separates the stuck from the transformed is this: Am I willing to let my life be poured out?

For many years I pursued a path of purity, growth, sanctification. I read my Bible and prayed. I forsook sin. I sought accountability. I made goals. I grew. But one day, as I sat in a corner of the local coffee shop, God gently revealed that in my passion and zeal for growth and sanctification, there was actually a subtle, selfish root: self-improvement.

In that moment, I realized that much of my tireless efforts at growth and change in the name of godliness was little more than selfish striving for self-improvement, masked in Jesus's name.

I had to ask myself, did I want a better life, or did I really want God? Did I want to stand taller, or was I willing to stoop lower? Did I want to just be proud of my accomplishments, or was I willing to be poured out? Did I want to be a spiritual self-improver or a genuine follower of Christ?

PICKED

In chapter 1, we saw that God's will for our lives is that we would bear fruit (John 15:8). We can do this no matter what our position or power, how much money we make or what limitations we face. The fruit is spiritual fruit: love, joy, peace, patience, kindness, goodness, gentleness, faithfulness, self-control. This is the fruit we are to bear. Just as we seek the health of a tree so that it will bear healthy fruit, we seek the health of our hearts, our inner person, so we will bear healthy fruit.

The question is, why does God want us to bear fruit? Well, why does a tree bear fruit? So it can admire itself? So it can stand tall and proud and look down at its fruit-laden limbs and say, "Wow, look at all my beautiful fruit! I should post pictures of it on Facebook"?

That's ridiculous, right? A tree bears fruit so the fruit can get picked. The whole point of a fruit tree is for folks to come along, pick, eat, and be nourished. And let's not forget where fruit comes from: flowers, which bring beauty to the world and silently witness to the glory of God.

A tree bears fruit so the fruit can get picked.

Remember, spiritual fruit is simply what God is. When we bear fruit, we're really just starting to look more like Jesus. We bear his image in greater measure, reflecting his glory and drawing others' eyes ultimately to him.

The twofold purpose of fruit: to bear witness to the beauty of God and to nourish those around us.

I propose that ministry is simply about getting "picked": we bear spiritual fruit and let others eat it. When someone comes to me with a need and I give generously with kindness and gentleness, that person is nourished and blessed in my presence. When my children are misbehaving and I train them with a spirit of patience instead of anger, I am ministering to them. When a difficult person is rude to me and I bear the fruit of self-control by holding my tongue instead of biting back with a sharp comment, I am ministering to that person. I am bearing fruit, nourishing that person, and displaying what God is like. My spiritual fruit bears witness to the glory of God and nourishes the spirits of all who are around me.

Our fruit was never meant to stay on the branch. Fruit that's left on the branch, unpicked, will rot. Personally, I hate to see this happen. Just last month I devoted whole days to picking and processing ninety pounds of plums, because I couldn't stand to see it stay up there on the tree, going to waste. In an infinitely greater way, unpicked spiritual fruit is a tragic waste of the Spirit's sacred work in our lives. Plus, it's not good for us! Picking fruit actually helps trees stay healthy. Not only does the world need to eat our fruit, but we ourselves benefit from getting picked. "Those who refresh others will themselves be refreshed" (Prov. 11:25 NLT). What blesses others will also bless us.

> ## Unpicked spiritual fruit is a tragic waste of the Spirit's sacred work in our lives.

I believe this is why we sometimes grow stagnant in our spiritual growth. We become unhealthy because we're not regularly getting picked. We make life goals and have high hopes for our spiritual transformation, but our aim is incomplete. We're wanting fruit for our own sake; we're wanting beautiful flowers only so we can look better. This won't work. Healthy trees can't carry selfie sticks. Healthy trees are healthy because they're busy handing out their fruit to a lost and lonely world.

What separates the world's New Year's resolutions from true spiritual transformation is who it's for and what we do with the results. Self-improvement is for us, and we use the results for us; true transformation seeks change and spiritual fruit for the glory of God and the good of others. We're wise to consider the difference and refuse to settle for anything less than God's greatest good in our lives.

JOYFUL POURING

Being picked and being poured out are two metaphors illustrating the same idea: letting our lives be emptied for the sake of Christ and for the good of those around us. And while this process certainly involves loss, Paul knew that it was the Christian's secret to joy. He insists, "Even if I am to be poured out as a drink offering upon the sacrificial offering of your faith, I am glad and rejoice with you all" (Phil. 2:17). This is a joyful pouring.

Paul knew that joy is found in living outside ourselves. He knew that abundant life wasn't found in endless navel gazing and self-improvement. He wasn't climbing higher and higher; he was bowing lower and lower.

Paul understood that joy is found not in personal development but in knowing Christ. He considered all things loss not for the sake of self-improvement, but for "the surpassing worth of knowing Christ" (Phil. 3:8). The more we get to know Christ, the more we realize our lostness and his greatness. We grow in lowness but also in joy.

The apostle reflected this understanding as he poured out his life in following Christ. First, Paul spoke of himself as "the least of the apostles" (1 Cor. 15:9). He walked in humility, considering the other apostles better than himself. Then as time went on, Paul said, "I am the very least of all the saints" (Eph. 3:8). What? Now he was not only the least of the apostles but also the least of all believers! Finally, at the end of his life, Paul called himself the chief of sinners (1 Tim. 1:15). He's not only the least of believers but the least of everybody!

This doesn't sound like the victorious Christian life, right? It sounds depressing. Not really, though. As Paul's self-estimation decreases, his joy increases. His faith increases. His spiritual strength increases. His *hupomone* increases. Paul continues to fight the good fight to the very end, accomplishing more than most of us could ever dream of. He knew a spiritual secret: our weakness unleashes God's strength.

Jesus was the same. Though he knew his identity as the Son of God, he "made himself nothing" for the sake of saving the world (Phil. 2:7 NIV). "For the *joy* set before him he endured the cross" (Heb. 12:2 NIV, emphasis mine), pouring out his life completely, more than any other, ever. He lost his life for us and considered it joy because he knew the blessed result. His disciples didn't understand why he would go to the cross. It looked like a waste, a defeat, a loss. But what looked like a waste to the world looked like worship to God, and the result was the redemption of the world.

WELL-WASTED POURING

Let's look at some women who lived this as well. One in particular stands out. She crept into the room quietly as all the important people bustled around, finding their favorite places. She knew she didn't belong there since she was a woman, but nothing could stop her. She took her precious alabaster flask of costly oil of spikenard. This was a year's wages, probably all she had. Her dowry, perhaps. Her only hope of marriage, of a future. Her reputation, her resources, her riches, all represented in this jar.

Then she does the unthinkable. She takes the jar, breaks it open, and pours it out on Jesus, anointing him. Worshipping him. Those around her are indignant. What is she doing? They argue, "Why this waste? This is equivalent to forty to fifty thousand dollars! This could have been sold and the money given to the poor."

That is a solid argument. Honestly, even a couple years ago I'd probably have been with the criticizers. But Jesus isn't. Jesus approves: "She has done a beautiful thing to me." And he goes on to commend her, saying her act of poured-out worship will be recounted throughout the whole world for all time (see Mark 14:3–9). And it is!

Giving to the poor is a good thing, so what is it that made this waste so beautiful to Jesus? I believe it is because it was truly for him. Nothing is wasted that is truly for Christ; everything is wasted that isn't. If what we give up is given *up* to him, it's worship.

Jesus knew their hearts, all of them, and he knows ours. It's easy to masquerade as philanthropists but still be secretly self-seeking. We can dress up our idols in churchy clothes. Jesus is the only one who truly sees the difference, and since he is the only one we aim to please, he's the only one who matters anyway.

Nothing is wasted that is truly for Christ; everything is wasted that isn't.

What motivated this woman to pour out all she had at Jesus's feet? She rightly valued Jesus above her reputation, her future, and her earthly treasures. Paul the apostle wrote, "Everything else is worthless when compared with the infinite value of knowing Christ Jesus my Lord. For his sake I have discarded everything else, counting it all as garbage, so that I could gain Christ" (Phil. 3:8 NLT). When we can say that with Paul, we'll be well on our way to true wealth.

This woman knew the truth: her waste was the wisest investment in the world.

UNMEASURED POURING

Let's consider this story from another angle. One might have analyzed this woman's outpouring and reasoned, "Hmm. It's too bad she was so rash. She could have carefully divvied up that oil. She could have given half away to the poor, saved a bit for her rainy-day fund, and still given a generous offering to Jesus." I know this sounds silly, but often this is how I reason. I'm a budgeter! I love me an Excel spreadsheet. Give me some rows and let's divvy stuff up!

This is fine for grocery budgets, but it isn't how worship works. This woman, commended by Jesus, didn't compartmentalize her life and carefully measure how much she wanted to give Jesus. She busted it all open and poured it out. Perhaps, we think, it's because she couldn't divide it. I've often heard it taught that it was impossible to open the flask without completely busting it open. But there's another woman in Scripture who does the same thing, when she could have easily divided and measured out just enough: the widow with her mites (Mark 12:41–44).

You know the story, right? She put two mites in the temple collection box.

I'm no whiz at math, but I know that two is divisible. I know that if I only had two coins to my name, and I wanted to give an offering to God, it wouldn't take much deliberation to determine that I would give one. That's 50 percent! That's still very generous. Still well above what's expected.

But this widow throws caution to the wind, forgets the Excel spreadsheet, leaves her calculator at home, and gives both coins.

The King James Version says she "threw in" her two mites. I love the image here. No hesitancy. No holding back. The same way that the first woman threw herself at Jesus's feet in worship, this widow threw in her whole livelihood as an offering to God. She poured out all she had.

Now, I'm not advocating that you empty your life savings and write a large check to your church. Maybe. That's between you and God. What I'm saying is that we can get so bogged down with measuring and calculating and tracking every jot and tittle of life, trying to figure out exactly how much we "have" to give to God, that we forget what it's all about: worship. I have heard Christ followers arguing over whether we're supposed to tithe off the gross or net income. Really? With all due respect, we are missing the point.

Even personally, I've wrestled with how much of the proceeds from this book to give away. Several years ago I sensed God saying, "All." I've gone back and forth. *Excuse me? Did I hear you right, Lord?* Again I hear, "All." That is, both mites. No need for percentages or careful calculations. Monetarily speaking it may be a tiny amount, a pittance, really, in the world's eyes. But to me it represents everything. My whole adult life I've been preparing to write this book; I've given it my all, and I'm giving *him* my all. It's a teeny-tiny way to say, "I love you, Jesus."

Jesus wants us to give because he wants us to love. Where our treasure is, our hearts will be (Luke 12:34). He wants our wholehearted, not halfhearted, worship. True worship isn't measured, calculated, tracked. Yes, God can and probably will speak to us specifically (down to the penny!) about how much money we are to give away, what he wants us to do with our time, how he wants us to minister, and so on. But that is all secondary.

He wants our wholehearted, not halfhearted, worship.

First, we pour it all out to him. We throw in both mites. We push all our chips to his side of the table. We say, "It's all yours, Jesus. *I* am all yours. My life is all yours. Do what you will with it, and with me. I love you."

This is what it means to "count" the cost. We rightly value what we gain (Christ) as infinitely greater than what we lose (self). Once we count the cost and follow Christ, we can go ahead and stop keeping track. It's all his. This is what it means to LET our lives be poured out.

Oh friends, I don't want to be the one standing back, arms folded, who goes through life measuring and calculating and critiquing others. I want to be the one busting open the jar, oblivious to the criticisms of those around, offering my all. You too? Then our lives will sing that last glorious stanza:

> Take my love, my Lord, I pour
> at Thy feet its treasure store.
> Take myself and I will be
> ever only all for Thee.
> —Frances Havergal,
> "Take My Life"

HIS PROMISED POURING

When we decide we want to pour out our lives for God, we are ready to receive a glorious promise: when we pour out, he pours down.

In Malachi 3, in the famous passage on tithing, God speaks to the

rebellious children of Israel because they have not been generously giving. He challenges them, "Bring the full tithe into the storehouse, that
there may be food in my house. And thereby put me to the test, says the
LORD of hosts, if I will not open the windows of heaven for you and *pour
down* for you a blessing until there is no more need" (Mal. 3:10, emphasis
mine).

God is not promising to fulfill every fancy of ours, but he is promising
to provide everything we truly need. When we pour out all we have, he
pours down all we need. Anne Frank said it well: "No one ever became
poor by giving."

When we pour out all we have, he pours down all we need.

It's true. God's promises are truer than the world's flawed logic, and
if we're done with the drunk goggles we will see clearly: when we pour
out, he pours down. If we are truly giving our lives to please God, not
just satisfy our pride or get a better tax rate or impress those around us,
then he will pour down all we need. Guaranteed. He will satisfy our
every need with himself. He will transform us. He will let our lives truly
flourish. That is the promise of Isaiah 58: "If you *pour yourself out* for the
hungry and satisfy the desire of the afflicted, then shall your light rise
in the darkness and your gloom be as the noonday. And the LORD will
guide you continually and satisfy your desire in scorched places and make
your bones strong; and you shall be like a watered garden, like a spring of
water, whose waters do not fail" (vv. 10–11, emphasis mine).

We all want to flourish, to thrive, and God tells us how: pour out.
Health and wholeness do not come from endless self-evaluation. Navel-
gazing leaves us with little more than a sore neck. True joy comes from
losing ourselves in pouring out our lives for the sake of others in worship
of God. C. S. Lewis has famously said, "The happiest moments are those
when we forget our precious selves."[1] As we *let* our lives be poured out,
God promises to pour into us the greatest gift: himself.

TIE YOURSELF

Now we reach the moment of decision. Are we ready to be poured out? Oswald Chambers describes this moment like this:

> Are you ready to be poured out as an offering? It is an act of your will, not your emotions. *Tell* God you are ready to be offered as a sacrifice for Him. Then accept the consequences as they come, without any complaints, in spite of what God may send your way.
> "Bind the sacrifice with cords to the horns of the altar" (Ps. 118:27). You must be willing to be placed on the altar and go through the fire; willing to experience what the altar represents—burning, purification, and separation for only one purpose—the elimination of every desire and affection not grounded in or directed toward God. But *you* don't eliminate it, God does. You "bind the sacrifice . . . to the horns of the altar" and see to it that you don't wallow in self-pity once the fire begins. After you have gone through the fire, there will be nothing that will be able to trouble or depress you. When another crisis arises, you will realize that things cannot touch you as they used to do. . . . Tell God you are ready to be poured out as an offering, and God will prove Himself to be all you ever dreamed He would be.[2]

As we close our time together, the question for us is, *Am I ready to climb up on the altar? Am I ready to present my body as a living sacrifice?* My friend Jessica says, "The problem with a living sacrifice is that it's always wiggling off the altar." Ha! Isn't that the truth! We experience some spiritual high and we stand, arms raised, and tearfully offer ourselves as God's willing servant forever. "Take my life!" we sing to him. And that's great.

But then we get home, and the kids are whinier than ever, and God calls you to apologize to your mother-in-law, and to forgive a friend for a long-ago hurt, and to stay quiet when you want to speak your mind, and to give up something that has been a part of you for longer than you can remember. We feel the fire and *yikes*! That fire is hot. We didn't realize the fire was going to hurt like that. It feels like real fire!

Yes, it does. Dying always feels like dying and fire is always hot. Maybe that's why Psalm 118:27 says to "bind the festal sacrifice with cords." You have to tie yourself up there. We are wise to note our tendency to wiggle off when the fire begins. That is why we decide once and for all that we are going to tie ourselves up there on that altar and *let* God pour us out as a living sacrifice. This means we "tie ourselves" to this decision.

It means I get up every morning, despite my screaming flesh that begs me for more sleep, and dig into God's Word and war in prayer, ditching the drunk goggles and choosing to align my heart and life with *God's* heart and life.

It means I gather with my local church family every week without exception. Unless I am unconscious or out of the country, I will not give up the habit of gathering together with the body of Christ, using my spiritual gifts to build up others, serve my brothers and sisters in Christ, and sit under the teaching of the Word, no matter how unspectacular a particular service or sermon may be. I will reject my flesh's constant craving for amusement and affirmation and embrace the community right in front of me, especially "the one" he has sovereignly placed in my path.

It means I meet with a few friends regularly, friends who tenaciously pursue my greatest good above my temporary pleasure, friends with whom I can be brutally honest about my struggles, friends who will steadfastly pursue godliness and holiness, friends who will help me tie myself to the altar and remind me of the goodness and glory of Jesus.

And it means I schedule generous giving to various sources, and read about real needs in other countries, exposing myself and my family regularly to the plight of others around the world, because if I leave it up to a whim, I will spend my finances all on myself. In this way, I tie myself to the altar.

Letting our lives be poured out is an act of the will. Our feelings will come and go. There will be days when I want nothing more than to ditch the path of self-denial. I never feel like fasting. Hardly ever do I feel like spending our spare money on mosquito nets rather than mochas. My spirit does, but my flesh gets obnoxiously loud some days and lures me off the altar, so it helps immensely if I'm securely tied down in various ways.

We must tie ourselves to the altar now, while it's relatively easy, because Scripture tells us there are days ahead when it will get hard.

THE LAST LEG

Several years ago I ran in the world's longest relay race, Hood-to-Coast. Our team was named "Girls and Guys with Aching Thighs," and this was an apt description! It was an incredible experience, spending thirty hours in a van with six other sweaty runners, sleeping on the ground, running in the middle of the night, becoming fast friends in that surprisingly immediate way that only a really uncomfortable circumstance can bring. There were twelve of us who ran three legs each, and I had the joy of being the last runner. This meant I ran the final stretch of the entire 200-mile race, stepping off pavement and onto sand, through the finish line.

I'll never forget the feeling of finishing well, and the key was, I knew when the end of the race was near.

See, each leg of the race had a map, complete with elevation and course description. I had studied my routes. I knew that last one—how it would climb for a straight mile, then drop steeply at the end, then wind through the city of Seaside, then end up on the beach.

When I reached the steep descent, I knew it was time to pour it all out. My quads hurt so bad. Our team name wasn't cute then—this was killin' me! But there was no use holding back, no reason to save strength for later. I knew I'd never regret giving it my all. I ran as hard as I could.

When I saw the ocean, I can't describe the joy in my heart. The view would have been breathtaking, but my breath was already taken. Thousands of people crowded on the beach, congratulating each other, an overwhelming celebration. What a glorious end! My team was there too, my beloved friends, cheering me on through those final strides off the sidewalk and onto the sand and through the finish line. I was tired but overjoyed. I was glad I had given it my all. So glad I'd poured out.

Friends, we're on the last leg.

I've been trying to think of a poetic way to put this and I can't, so I'll just say it: Jesus is returning. Like, *soon*. Believe me, I am the furthest thing from an eschatology-obsessed, reading-Revelation-over-and-over, stockpiling-supplies-for-Armageddon kind of girl. Okay? I have zero interest in end-time arguments and pre-trib or post-trib camps. This isn't the time to huddle together under banners Jesus didn't wave. Jesus did give us some pretty specific instruction, however, and one of the most repeated was simply this: know the signs of the times.

> This isn't the time to huddle together under banners Jesus didn't wave.

Throughout the Gospels, Jesus exhorts us, "Stay awake." He warns us that just as in the days of Noah, the end will come upon many when they least expect it. He gives us many clues to help discern when his return is near, a course map, so to speak, and although no one knows the day, we do know the season. We have a pretty clear description of the last leg. And Jesus says explicitly, "When these things begin to take place, straighten up and raise your heads, because your redemption is drawing near" (Luke 21:28).

Friends, our full redemption is drawing near. As I have been praying about this chapter, asking specifically what God wanted me to say, I heard this simple phrase over and over in my heart: "Tell them I'm coming soon."

So there. Jesus is coming soon. I have no definition of what "soon" is, but there is no way I'm ignoring this sense in my spirit, and I have seen dozens of things lining up recently that convince me our time here is coming to a close. I've seen the course description of this final stretch. There's a steep descent upon us, and it's moments before the ocean opens up before us and we see the finish line.

These are the days for pouring out.

In the book of James, God gives a harsh indictment of the rich because they hoarded their resources instead of pouring them out for others. Specifically, James writes, "You have laid up treasure in the last days" (James 5:3). In other words, this is the time to pour out, not store up. Now is not the time to lay up treasures here on earth. Now is not the time to hold back, saving some for later.

These are the last days, a time for all to pour out, and our glorious God has promised to go first.

OUTPOURING

God is always previous, so he pours out first. And he is doing so. We are seeing unprecedented outpouring of his Spirit on this earth in prophecy and signs, in miracles and movements. And we are also seeing increasing darkness. We are seeing the chasm grow wide and the gradual separation between opposing kingdoms. It's becoming increasingly difficult to live lukewarm, and the fence won't hold us up any longer. We have to pick a side. Those who choose Christ are given a precious and great promise: "In the last days, God says, I will pour out my Spirit on all people . . . and everyone who calls on the name of the Lord will be saved" (Acts 2:17, 21 NIV).

He's been calling us to bear fruit, and it's nearing harvest time. Let's bring this full circle. My desire is that we would let our days transform our lives. That we'd dip down into our ordinary days in such a way that we are radically transformed from the inside out. That our mind-sets change, our habits change, our marriages change, our budgets change, our lives change. That we would find freedom, unwavering purpose, and unquenchable joy. Why? So we can bear fruit that nourishes those near and far and displays God's glory for all to see. This is how we prepare for every ordinary Tuesday, and this is how we prepare for the glorious return of Christ. Jesus already promised he will commend those who were faithful with little, so our simple aim is to live our sacred mundane in a way that pleases him.

One key to this was learning to let *hupomone* have its work in our lives. Through our mundane suffering, *hupomone* is produced in us, leading to character change (transformation), leading to hope. And hope is the difference between us and the world. We who are Christ followers have an eternal hope, and this hope is what we offer the reeling world he loves.

Hupomone is needed for more than just our daily household tasks—it is what we need to finish well. Humanity's longest relay race runs from creation to Christ's return. Each generation runs a portion; each person runs a leg. We pass the baton of faith on down and make disciples who, coming after us, will run even stronger, faster, and more faithfully than we did. We don't know exactly how it ends, but we do know that some folks will be running the final portion. Jesus outlines this in Luke 21. After giving the course description of what our last leg will look like, he gives some sobering warnings about difficult days ahead, then leaves us with this: "By your endurance [*hupomone*] you will gain your lives" (Luke 21:19).

Humanity's longest relay race runs from creation to Christ's return. Each generation runs a portion; each person runs a leg.

No matter how hairy things get here on earth, *hupomone* will carry us through. *Hupomone* will uphold us when our hearts fail, when the world feels scary, when circumstances feel out of control. *Hupomone* will keep us tied to the altar when we're increasingly tempted to wiggle off and join the comfortable crowd out in the world. *Hupomone* will continue to produce hope in our lives, which we will need in ever-increasing measure as the world grows darker and our lights shine brighter. Jesus said that in the end, the love of many would grow cold (Matt. 24:12). *Hupomone* will help our hearts stay hot.

And as we run the race with *hupomone*, giving it all we've got, we will lift our eyes and "straighten up and lift up your heads, because your redemption is drawing near" (Luke 21:28 NASB).

We'll get a glimpse of the ocean and all else will fade away. Aching quads won't matter. Blisters won't matter. Burning lungs won't matter. The real finish line will be glorious.

I want you to get to the end with no regrets, friends. I want to pour out my life to help you prepare to meet your Creator. I want to do all I can to help prepare the bride to meet her Groom, King Jesus. I want you to be spotless, dipping down deep into your dirty days, and emerging to find yourself whole, healed, clean.

It is through pouring out that we will be prepared to meet him.

By our *hupomone* we will gain our lives.

There is no need to despise these ordinary days. These dirty waters, they are working for us. They are preparing us, equipping us, readying us. This is not a game. Jesus himself is knocking on the door of our lives, and if we will *let* him in, he will come and make something glorious out of our mundane. He will change our sentences, one *but* at a time, writing redemption's story with our rewritten lives, weaving us into his glorious plan to draw all people to himself. With those from every tongue, tribe, and nation, we will join together to worship our King, and I believe we will glance back at life and be amazed at all the ways our seemingly insignificant moments mattered.

We will be glad we stopped, stooped, and spoke gently to the woman on the street. We will be glad we made that tiny choice that no one else saw to deny ourselves and give away. We will be glad we turned down the voice of the world and tuned in to the still, small voice of our Lord. We will be glad we stuck with that difficult relationship when we so desperately wanted to give up. I believe we will just be deliriously happy at the end that we poured out our lives, that we risked it all, sold the farm, and bought the field with the hidden treasure of God.

This is both tiny and huge. It's a mustard seed that grows into a mountain. We start small, learning to LOOK at the world through the Word, interpreting life God's way. We LISTEN to his voice, discerning his direction and learning his heart. We ENGAGE, dipping down and getting wet, refusing to escape, letting the hard moments move us forward.

We EMBRACE "the one" God has placed in our path. We TRUST God with our blanks, stepping out into the nothingness, learning to walk by faith. And we THANK him in the midst, choosing expectancy over expectation, clinging to his promises more than to our picture plans, and witnessing his glorious fulfillment in our lives. He is so good.

Begin today. Dip down deep into *your* sacred mundane; and by the grace of God, for the glory of God, LET your days transform your life.

Acknowledgments

———◆———◆———◆———

Jeff. There just aren't words. My life has been forever changed by your love. You have loved me at my most unlovable. You have nurtured me with kindness. You have fanned faith into flame when I have most wanted to give up. None of this would be if it weren't for you. You are the gospel lived out in front of me every day. I love you beyond words. Thank you.

Dutch and Heidi, my squirrels! Thank you for your patience over five years of bringing this book into being; I know it felt like forever! Thank you for endless hours snuggled up beside me while I typed and for your faithful prayers. Dutch, thanks for celebrating with me when the manuscript was finished. Heidi, thanks for drawing your own cover. I love you.

Mom and Dad, you have laid down your lives for me. I have no idea why I was blessed with the most incredible parents in the world, but I am eternally grateful. Mom, thank you for praying me into God's good plan. Dad, thank you for showing me the Father.

The team! Elisa, Caila, Joanna, Candi, Grace, Anne, Christine, Elisha, Linda, Janae, Kimmee, Danielle, Molly, Debra, Rachel, Janie: you are the doulas! Your faithful prayers, support, and encouragement have birthed this book baby into existence. It would not be here if it weren't for you. Thank you for being my friends.

Cak'em! Insert a million heart-eye emojis here.

David Sanford, a gift from God. Providence placed me in your publishing workshop that year at FCWC, and I am forever grateful! Thank you for taking a huge risk and devoting so much time and energy to this little girl's big dream. You've been like a father to me. Thank you for protecting and promoting me, for praying this book into existence, and for not giving up even when I wanted to. Kregel, thank you for being a joy to work with. Janyre and Bob, you are geniuses!

Most of all, thank you, Jesus, for saving my soul and giving me life. I love you desperately and pray this little book makes you smile. I will worship you forever; you are so good.

Small Group Bible Study

LET the Word Come to Life

HELLO! I'M SO GLAD you've decided to take this journey toward transformation. I hope you've gathered a group of friends to walk alongside; it's always best to go this way together.

Please plan on gathering nine times, completing eight weeks of study materials. Before your first gathering, please read this book's introduction, "The Sentence of Your Life," and jot down your initial thoughts on the sentence of *your* life.

As you write, please keep this in mind: don't just write a sterile sentence that is "safe" to share. Spend some time in prayer, asking God to reveal any unseen areas that are hindering your joy, peace, victory, and freedom. Ask him to help you write a real sentence, even if it means you aren't comfortable sharing it with others. It's okay if you're uncomfortable. It may be that you'd like to continue wearing the turtleneck for a while, and it might take a few weeks to feel comfortable sharing in a group. That's fine. The most important thing is that you are dead-bang honest and transparent with God. Do whatever it takes to foster that honesty, even if it means you write out your sentence and then bury it in your yard so no one can see it. Just relax and do whatever works.

Lastly, let's agree to laugh at ourselves a bit and openly acknowledge that we all have spiritual leprosy in some way or another. Right? We've all got stuff. Moreover, we tend to stay stuck and bound by the struggles that are most embarrassing to admit. Let's push through that and reveal the "leprous skin," whatever the issue may be. This is the path to freedom, purpose, and joy! The fresh air of honesty is good for the soul.

Again, thank you so much for taking the time not only to read *Sacred Mundane* but also to study, consider, ponder, pray, and apply these truths to your life. I pray you will learn to LET your days transform your life. Let's begin!

Week 1
THE SENTENCE OF YOUR LIFE

- Take some time to go around and share some of the various "first halves" of your life sentences. That is, how has God wired you? What relationships, roles, and responsibilities define your days? What does your mundane look like?
- If anyone is feeling bold right off the bat, feel free to share the ways you think God desires to rewrite the sentence of your life. It always takes one brave soul to go first!
- Consider how Naaman brought his own resources into the situation, hoping his silver and gold would earn his healing. How do we tend to do this? In what ways do we try to bring our own elaborate plans or provision to a problem, showing God we are "really serious this time"?
- How is Naaman's story a perfect picture of the gospel? How are we all lost and leprous? How do we attempt to fix our issues on our own? How do we resist the call to come and die, to lay aside the filthy rags of our own righteousness, and dip down into the waters of salvation, the waters of life, receiving the free gift of Christ's perfect righteousness? Review "The Gospel of Naaman" below and take some time to consider whether you have truly received the free gift of God's saving grace. Surrender your own attempts at healing yourself or earning your own transformation. Leave the chariots and changes of clothes behind. Before you can dip down into your days you must dip down into the saving waters of Jesus Christ's finished work on the cross. Take some time together to revisit the power of the gospel, and commit to rest your hope solely on God's saving and transforming power. Finish in prayer, offering up this journey to God and asking for his leading and power in your lives.

The Gospel of Naaman

In the Scriptures, leprosy is a picture of sin. Naaman, then, is a perfect picture of the problem that every person on earth must eventually face. We're all leprous. No matter how neat and tidy our lives or how accomplished we may be, the Bible says that "all have sinned and fall short of the glory of God" (Rom. 3:23), that no one is righteous (v. 10). Because of Adam's initial disobedience, all of us were infected with sin (5:19), leaving us lost and incapable of approaching the presence of God. Then, not only were we infected by sin but we chose sin. We chose the turtlenecks, chose to go our own way, chose the path of self. Just as Adam and Eve hid in their shame, we too have hidden behind the robes of fear. We still tend to think we can do our own thing and it will work out okay.

But it doesn't. The leprosy lingers, grows, gets infected. We can't manage our lives with our own resources. The gold and silver and ten changes of clothes—they're really useless for curing incurable diseases. Our own capabilities are woefully incapable. Eventually there comes a time when we recognize, there is a God, and it's not me. So we, like Naaman, surrender. We leave behind all our own attempts at gaining salvation on our own terms. We dip down into the saving waters of Jesus Christ.

Jesus Christ was God's own Son, begotten by the Holy Spirit and birthed through Mary to bring salvation to earth. Jesus is the arm of God, reaching down to earth to gather up his lost children. Just as the sinless lambs were offered in the Old Testament as atonement for sin, Jesus came as the sinless Lamb of God who takes away the sins of the world (John 1:29). No longer do continual sacrifices have to be made over and over, but Jesus accomplished our salvation once and for all, when he breathed his last words, "It is finished" (Heb. 10:11–12; John 19:30). Then, in the most earth-shattering event of human history, God raised Jesus from the dead, conquering sin and death and proving his power over Satan. Though we are still promised tribulation in life, we're also told the end of the story: we win!

Jesus gave us a crystal-clear picture of what God is like (John 14:9). Jesus only did the will of the Father, and he operated not in his own strength but in God the Father's. He showed us what fully redeemed humanity looks like, demonstrating authority over every effect of the fall by calming storms, healing disease, raising the dead, forgiving sin, feeding the hungry, and preaching the good news that the free gift of salvation is extended to all.

But each of us must actively receive that salvation. We cannot stand on the shore and think saving thoughts. We cannot send our spouse or our friend into the water for us. We cannot choose our own waters, thinking we can determine our own path to God. There is only one God and one Savior, Jesus Christ (1 Tim. 2:5). He is the only path to God. He is the way, the truth, and the life. No one comes to the Father but through him (John 14:6).

Each of us must choose. Each of us must leave behind our own righteousness and dip completely down into waters of Christ, fully surrendering our whole lives to him and giving over control to him as King.

This is how we are saved. And our salvation is bigger and better than we ever dared dream. It extends to every ounce and aspect of our being. His salvation and our subsequent sanctification (the process of becoming like Christ) bring physical, emotional, and spiritual health and wholeness. It's a lifelong process, but it's a good and worthwhile journey away from sin and selfishness and into abundant life.

And finally, as if this weren't good news enough, how the gospel gives new life to us now, we are also given the promise of eternal life, of living forever with God: "He will wipe away every tear from their eyes, and death shall be no more, neither shall there be mourning, nor crying, nor pain anymore, for the former things have passed away" (Rev. 21:4).

This is the gospel of Naaman. This is the invitation. Come, dive deep into this grace; come take the life-plunge into the life, death, and resurrection of Jesus Christ, the water of salvation for our souls.

Week 2
LET HIM IN

Day 1: Read—Chapter 1
- Read chapter 1 of *Sacred Mundane*. Highlight text and jot down your thoughts along the way so you'll be ready to discuss with your group.
- Write out James 1:4 on a notecard. Review daily and commit to memory.

Day 2: Read—Responses and Reactions to Christ
- Read Matthew 4:18–22; 8:18–22; 19:16–22; Mark 1:16–20; 2:13–14; 6:1–6; 8:11–13, 27–30; 10:17–22; 14:50; Luke 4:22–30; 5:27–28; 9:18–20; 18:18–29; John 1:35–50; 6:66–69; 21:15–19. (Tip: You can type these all into a Bible Gateway search and see them all listed together.)
- List the different characters mentioned and how they responded to Jesus in each situation. If they let him in (received and followed him), what did it cost them? What was the reward? If they rejected him, why? If they were offended at him, how so? Why do responses and reactions to Jesus vary so wildly?
- Review James 1:4.

Day 3: Reflect—LET Him In
- Reflecting on the passages from yesterday, put yourself in the shoes of each character. How might you have responded in each of the situations?
- Write your own scene. Don't worry about grammar or style; just write out, as best as you can, what the scene of your life is right now. Where are you at, spiritually speaking? What is your environment like? Where is Jesus showing himself or inserting himself into the

scene, and how are you responding? What is he saying to you? What is he calling you to? How are you reacting? Are there any ways you are afraid to let him in?

- As an act of faith, finish your scene/story by writing out what it would look like for you to completely surrender and whole-heartedly let Jesus into your life—your real life. Be as specific as possible.
- Think about the various people you let into your home. How does their presence impact the climate? Do you prepare for their arrival? If so, how? How do you feel after they leave?
- If Jesus came in person to your home today, how do you think it would impact your daily life? Are there any aspects of your mundane, everyday life that you wouldn't want him to see? Any rooms or closets in your home or heart? Your Internet history? Your credit card statement? Journal a few sentences identifying any areas you want to welcome Christ more fully into your mundane.
- Review James 1:4.

Day 4: Read—Sacrifice, Suffering, and Spiritual Strength
- Read Romans 5:3; 12:1–2; 2 Corinthians 4:17–18; Hebrews 13:15–16; James 1:3–4.
- In your own words, answer and explain the following. Be as practical and specific as possible, avoiding "Christianese." (Think of how you would explain these things to someone who has no biblical background.)
    - What is the difference between a sacrifice of atonement and a sacrifice of praise? What is the purpose of a sacrifice? What did Christ's sacrifice accomplish? What does ours accomplish?
    - What does it mean that our bodies are a living sacrifice?
    - What is *hupomone* and how is it produced?
    - How does suffering work for us? What sort of perspective is critical for this process to be effective?
- Review James 1:4.

Day 5: Reflect—You, a Sacred Offering

- Spend some time in prayer considering Romans 12:1–2 (read the passage several times and focus on its truths as you pray), asking God to show you what it means, specifically, to offer your body as a living sacrifice to him. Ask him to show you if there are any areas that aren't pleasing to him, any areas where you are being conformed to this world rather than transformed. Confess (agree with him) if he identifies a sin area. There isn't anything to "show" for this exercise; the goal is to spend time interacting intimately with God in complete honesty and transparency. If prayer times such as this are new to you, start with five minutes of uninterrupted quiet time with your Father.
- Review James 1:4.

Day 6: Respond—Clean Out, Work Out

- Choose one physical area of your home (or life) that reflects disorder or dysfunction. It could be a closet, a drawer, your car, anything. The point is to tie mental and spiritual strings between our daily mundane and our spiritual growth. Today, tackle this area. Clean, organize, or make a plan for bringing this small physical space under control (under your lordship) as you bring your whole life under Christ's lordship. Pray as you complete this physical task. Ask God to show you any parallels between the physical state of this space and the spiritual state of your heart. (Hint: Choose a small, relatively easy space you can complete in one day!)
- Work out your muscles in some physical way. If you have weights, lift them. If not, use cans of food or try push-ups. Remember, we all have different capabilities, so be realistic about yours. Of course, if you're an athlete, use enough weight that you can feel the burn. Be creative and do something that makes your muscles fatigued, praying as you do that God would strengthen you spiritually and help you press through when you "feel the burn" in life. Thank him for the hand weights he gives us that work *hupomone* into our lives.
- Review James 1:4.

Day 7: Discussion

Today, as you gather with your group, discuss the following questions:

- What struck you most from chapter 1 of *Sacred Mundane*?
- What's one thing you remember from the Scripture reading for day 2? Whose response to Jesus was most interesting to you? Why?
- If you're comfortable, describe the scene you wrote on day 3. What is the spiritual scene in your life right now? How is Christ inserting himself there, and how are you responding?
- Read your definitions from day 4. Were there any new insights you had as you looked up those Scriptures and wrote out the answers in your own words?
- Did you clean out that area of your home? What did you learn or discover as you prayerfully completed this task? Did you exercise your muscles? How did that feel?
- Going forward, is there one specific act of obedience Christ is calling you to this next week?

Additional Reading

The Practice of the Presence of God by Brother Lawrence
The Everyday Gospel by Tim Chester

Week 3
LOOK: SEE THE WORLD THROUGH THE WORD

Day 1: Read—Chapter 2
- Read chapter 2 of *Sacred Mundane*.
- Write out 2 Corinthians 4:17–18 on a notecard. Review daily and commit to memory.

Day 2: Read—Receive God's Lens
- Read Luke 8:4–15. How does this parable illustrate how we are to receive the Word of God? What conditions are important to receive well, so that our lives bear spiritual fruit? Of the dangers listed, which one poses the most significant threat to you personally?
- In your own words, how would you explain the difference between reading and receiving?
- Read Romans 12:2. How does this verse sum up the idea of the world's "drunk goggles" and our need to put on the clear lens of God's Word?
- Review 2 Corinthians 4:17–18.

Day 3: Reflect—Ditching the Drunk Goggles
- Spend some time in prayer asking God to reveal any areas where the world's drunk goggles have distorted your vision and given you a skewed perspective. Think through some of the current challenging circumstances in your life, and ask God to show you specifically how he sees each situation. Ask him to lead you to any Scriptures that would shed light on a given situation. Journal your thoughts.
- Review 2 Corinthians 4:17–18.

Day 4: Read—His Powerful Word
- Read Psalms 19:7; 119:105; Jeremiah 15:16; Matthew 4:4; John 17:17;

Acts 20:32; Romans 1:16; 10:17; Colossians 3:16; 2 Timothy 3:16–17; Hebrews 4:12; James 1:22; 1 Peter 1:23. Next to each passage, jot down a brief answer to this question: What does this say about the power of God's Word? Then, in your own words, explain the importance of a believer's remaining in the Word of God.

- Review 2 Corinthians 4:17–18.

Day 5: Reflect—Let His Word Dwell in You

- Without comparing yourself to anyone else, and laying aside any sense of *should*, ask God humbly and honestly how he wants you to regularly receive his Word. Ask him for eyes to see clearly, and honestly evaluate whether his Word is dwelling in you. Ask him to reveal any other sources you turn to on a regular basis instead of turning to him as the true source. Ask him what he wants your devotional life to look like. Check out the link in the additional reading below with many helpful Bible reading plans. Ask him to lead you specifically: pick a time, a place, and a plan. Jot down your thoughts on how you can let your mind be more and more transformed by increasing your intake of God's mind-transforming Word.
- Review 2 Corinthians 4:17–18.

Day 6: Respond—Practice Seeing the World Through the Word

- Take a moment to intentionally "look" at the world. Consider the books you read, shows you watch, magazines you enjoy, Internet sites you visit, blogs you follow. Or read billboards while driving, or briefly peruse something on TV or an online publication. Take a few moments to write your answers to the following:
  - ★ What is the world's "gospel" that is being preached, and what is the contrasting truth of God's Word? Specifically, how might the world's message bring distortion, leading to one's downfall?
  - ★ What are some of the common messages presented most often to you and your family? What is the danger of these distorted messages, and how does God's Word bring clarity and truth?

   ★ In what practical ways can you combat this distortion by actively abiding in God's Word, seeing clearly and helping your family to do so as well? Be specific.

- Review 2 Corinthians 4:17–18.

Day 7: Discussion

Today, as you gather with your group, we'll be discussing the following questions. Take a few moments now to look over this week's study and refresh your mind on what God has spoken to you and done in your heart.

- Considering the parable of the seeds, what do you think are the birds or sun or weeds in your own soil? In other words, what things prevent God's Word from bearing fruit?
- As you are comfortable, share some of your current challenges or frustrations and any way God revealed his perspective to you as you considered them through the lens of his Word.
- What aspect of God's powerful Word most struck you from day 4? How does this impact your day-to-day life?
- Are there ways group members can hold you accountable to what God showed you on day 5 with regard to your receiving his Word in your devotional life? How can the rest of the group help you successfully obey in this area?
- Which of the world's messages did you discover yesterday? How do you see them impacting your family? What is the truth that brings clear vision?

Additional Reading

Women of the Word by Jen Wilkin

Bible reading plans: http://www.backtothebible.org/bible-reading-guides.html

Week 4
LISTEN: DISCERN HIS VOICE IN DAILY LIFE

Day 1: Read—Chapter 3

- Read chapter 3 of *Sacred Mundane*. Highlight text and jot down your thoughts along the way so you'll be ready to discuss with your group.
- Write out 1 Thessalonians 5:17 on a notecard. Review daily and commit to memory.

Day 2: Read—Paul's Prayers

- Read Paul's prayers in 1 Corinthians 1:4–8; Ephesians 1:15–23; 4:14–21; Philippians 1:9–11; 1 Thessalonians 3:11–13; 2 Thessalonians 1:11–12; 2:16–17; 3:5; Philemon 1:4–6. Write out the various things for which Paul prays. What strikes you most about each? Which aspect of Paul's prayers will you incorporate more into your own?
- Review 1 Thessalonians 5:17.

Day 3: Reflect—The Invitation

- Is there any way you haven't grasped or appreciated the greatness of the invitation to prayer? Has fear or cynicism or unbelief crept in, keeping you from engaging in the most life-giving interaction you can have and wielding the most powerful weapon? Take a few moments and ask God to reveal to you the greatness of this invitation. Journal your thoughts, struggles, hesitations, fears. In what ways do you feel like a failure in prayer? In what aspects of it do you long to grow? What obstacles do you face?
- Practice today talking openly and honestly with your heavenly Father, out loud, expressing your mixed emotions to him and asking him to teach you to pray.
- Review 1 Thessalonians 5:17.

Day 4: Read—Jesus Teaches Us to Pray

- Read Matthew 6:5–15 and Luke 11:1–13. What observations can you make from Jesus's teaching on prayer? What from these passages applies to your current journey of growing in prayer (based on what you wrote yesterday)? What part of Jesus's teaching most challenges you?
- Use this link (http://bit.ly/hupomone) to look up the verses about endurance. What observations can you make? (Better yet, jot down the references and look them up in your Bible so you can underline and make notes in the margins.)
- Use this link (http://bit.ly/makrothumia) to look up the verses about patience, making observations and noting any insights that come to mind.
- Review 1 Thessalonians 5:17.

Day 5: Reflect—Childlike

- How did it strike you to reflect on prayer as a conversation between a child and her Father? What childlike qualities most stood out to you, and which would most benefit your interactions with God? For example, do you need to stop pretending and begin where you are? Do you need to pray out loud? How does your view of God as your Father impact your desire to commune with him? Journal through these questions, reflecting on any hesitations you feel about total openness with God. Ask him to teach you to pray and to draw your heart toward his.
- Of the three hindrances to hearing, which do you think most applies to you at this moment? How, specifically, might God want more of your attention in the midst of the mundane?
- Review 1 Thessalonians 5:17.

Day 6: Respond—Practice Discerning His Voice in Daily Life

- Today, practice hearing God's voice. Perhaps set a timer to chime each hour, reminding you to draw your attention upward, giving simple thanks or asking for strength. Or simply breathe a quick prayer, such as, "Lord, teach me to pray," or "I love you, Father. Draw my heart to yours." Choose something simple that you can whisper in one breath to God throughout the day, increasing your awareness of him in the midst of the mundane. If you have kids, include them! Explain that you are practicing the presence of God, and invite them to join you in age-appropriate ways. Be sure to jot down your thoughts. At the end of the day, reflect on its challenges and joys as you practiced ceaseless prayer. What did you hear God say?

- Review 1 Thessalonians 5:17.

Day 7: Discussion

Today, as you gather with your group, we'll be discussing the following questions. Take a few moments to look over this week's study and refresh your mind on what God has spoken to you and done in your heart.

- What struck you most about Paul's prayers? Was there anything you intentionally incorporated into your own prayers?
- As you are comfortable, consider sharing how you would describe your current prayer life and how you most desire to grow. Is there someone in your group (or in your life) whom you might ask for accountability, or whom you might pray with regularly so you both will grow?
- What struck you from Jesus's teaching on prayer and your study of *hupomone* and *makrothumia*? Which of these qualities do you need most right now?
- How did yesterday go, practicing God's presence throughout your day? What challenges did you face? What victories and joys did you experience?

Additional Reading

A Praying Life by Paul Miller

Prayer: Finding the Heart's True Home by Richard Foster

Week 5
ENGAGE: ENTER IN

Day 1: Read—Chapter 4

- Read chapter 4 of *Sacred Mundane*. Highlight text and jot down your thoughts along the way so you'll be ready to discuss with your group.
- Write out 1 Corinthians 10:31 on a notecard. Review daily and commit to memory.

Day 2: Read—Mundane Matters

- Read 1 Timothy 3:4–5. What connection does Paul make between "mundane" duties at home and "sacred" responsibilities in the church? In what ways are we tempted to divide sacred and secular activities, behaving differently at different times? Spend some time asking God if there is any separation between your "sacred" life and your "secular" life, any lack of integrity, that isn't pleasing to him.
- Read Ephesians 4:29; Colossians 4:5; 1 Thessalonians 4:10–12; 2 Thessalonians 3:10–12; 1 Timothy 2:9–10; 6:6–8; Titus 2:3–5. What mundane aspects of life are emphasized in these passages, and how are we called to worship and obey God in these everyday details of life?
- Review 1 Corinthians 10:31.

Day 3: Reflect—Worshipful Work

- What different jobs have you had? What was your attitude toward each one? How did you enter into the setting? Whom did you learn from? What was challenging? What did you learn from each of these experiences? How have they shaped who you are today?
- What is your work now—that is, on a daily basis, what do you do? How do you engage in it, fully entering in? How is your attitude?

What about your work is challenging? What are you learning? How is it worship? How might you more fully enter into it as a praise offering to God?

- Review 1 Corinthians 10:31.

Day 4: Read—Remain

- Read 1 Timothy 1:3–7. Why did Paul tell Timothy to remain in Ephesus? Considering the rest of the passage, what was going on? Why would it have been easier for Timothy to check out, give up, and move on? Are there any situations in your life where it would be easier for you to do that—someone or something you're tempted to write off or give up on? Over what aspect of your life do you wish you could click "delete"? How might this situation be the key to your transformation? How can you enter into this situation and let God work in and through you?
- Review 1 Corinthians 10:31.

Day 5: Reflect—Engage

- Consider Romans 12:15: "Rejoice with those who rejoice, weep with those who weep." Is there anyone in your life who is experiencing significant joys or sorrows you might enter into with them? Prayerfully consider how, specifically, you can bless a loved one with your presence by entering into that person's emotions and experiences. Ask God for his holy creativity and direction.
- Review 1 Corinthians 10:31.

Day 6: Respond—Refuse Escape

- How are you tempted to escape the pressures of daily life instead of entering in? Ask God to show you any escape routes that neither please him nor refresh and strengthen your spirit. As you practice his presence today, ask him to identify points in your day when you are most likely to escape. What unhelpful outlets do you turn to? Media? Food? How do they short-circuit what God may want to do

in your life, and what can you do instead? Putting away your cell phone, closing the pantry, setting down the magazine . . . whatever ideas God gives you, obey him and engage fully in the day ahead.
- Review 1 Corinthians 10:31.

Day 7: Discussion

Today, as you gather with your group, we'll be discussing the following questions. Take a few moments to look over this week's study and refresh your mind on what God has spoken to you and done in your heart.

- What was the most challenging or frustrating job you've ever had? Why? What did you learn through it? How did you see God work in your life through it?
- Where in your life do you desire greater cohesion and wholeness? Where are you most tempted to divide sacred and secular? Is there any place God highlighted this week where he wants to bring more wholeness?
- How are you tempted to escape a difficult situation? How might the Lord be exhorting you to "remain in _____!" Fill in the blank, and share how you intend to stick out the situation by faith.
- Whom can you empathize with? Who came to mind on day 5? How were you able to engage with this person? What did you discover in the process?
- How did yesterday go, refusing to escape? What ways are you tempted to escape? What challenges and victories did you experience?

Additional Reading

The Pursuit of God by A. W. Tozer

Week 6
EMBRACE: LOVE THE ONE

Day 1: Read—Chapter 5

- Read chapter 5 of *Sacred Mundane*. Highlight text and jot down your thoughts along the way so you'll be ready to discuss with your group.
- Write out 1 John 3:18 on a notecard. Review daily and commit to memory.

Day 2: Read—The Heart of the Gospel

- Read Isaiah 53:2–6; John 13:34–35; 15:12–13; Romans 5:8; 1 John 3:11–18; 4:7–21. Jot down key observations on each passage as it concerns the love of the Savior and the essence of the gospel. How is love at the very heart of the gospel? How would you explain the gospel succinctly to someone who has never heard it?
- Review 1 John 3:18.

Day 3: Reflect—Why the Mundane Matters

- Reread C. S. Lewis's quote from page 98. How does this quote strike you? In everyday life, how do we tend to lose our view of eternity and the reality that each person is an immortal soul? Journal your thoughts.
- On a daily basis, how do you see yourself "helping others along" toward one of the two destinations mentioned? Besides the more overt ways, such as proclaiming the gospel with words, by what other subtle ways are you influencing others in your life? Do you have a "Penielle" in your life—someone you are called to love who challenges you as well? How can you help this person experience the love of God?
- Review 1 John 3:18.

Day 4: Read—How Love Becomes Real

- Read Luke 10:25–37. How might each of the four main characters—priest, Levite, Samaritan, victim—have viewed the situation? In what ways do you identify with the priest or the Levite? How was the Good Samaritan's heroism rather normal? In what ways do you sometimes overlook the ordinary, mundane ways you can help others every day? In what areas do you feel discouraged or tempted to quit because your actions seem too insignificant to matter?
- Read 1 John 3:17–18 and James 2:8–26. How do love and faith become real? Journal any observations or things that strike you from these passages.

Day 5: Reflect—Keep Yourself from Idols

- Which of the four main idols of the heart (p. 113) most strikes you? Spend time in prayer asking God to show you which idol your heart is most prone toward. Converse with your loving Father about any ways he wants to lead you, his little child, in keeping yourself from idols (1 John 5:21). Make sure to journal!
- Review 1 John 3:18.

Day 6: Respond—Love in Deed

- Thinking back to 1 John 3:17, consider these three questions:
  - ★ What do you have? ("If anyone has the world's goods . . .") The freeing truth is that God doesn't call us to give anything we don't have! What's in your hand? What do you possess? What power do you have?
  - ★ Whom do you see? ("and sees his brother in need . . .") Again, this is freeing! We are responsible for what we see. We must pay attention to providence. Whom has God sovereignly placed in your path?
  - ★ What will you do? ("yet closes his heart . . .") Scripture equates acting with love. What prayerful, purposeful action will you take?

- Spend some time now asking God for his specific instruction on how to actively love the one he has given you today. Who comes to mind when you think of "the one"? Journal your thoughts (for your eyes only), including any wrestling or challenges surrounding this issue. Ask God to show you one concrete way to love the one in your life, not in word only but in deed and truth. There is no "right" action other than the one God tells you to do. Take whatever practical step he asks of you today. If time allows, journal about it afterward.
- Review 1 John 3:18.

Day 7: Discussion

Today, as you gather with your group, we'll be discussing the following questions. Take a few moments to look over this week's study and refresh your mind on what God has spoken to you and done in your heart.

- How does the love of God compel us? In every area of our lives, how is it the love of God that forms, informs, and fuels everything we do? Why must we constantly return to the love of God as our anchor?
- From day 4, are there any ways you are currently seeking to love others, but it doesn't feel significant or worth it? Are there any areas in which you are becoming discouraged in your efforts to love? How can we pray for you?
- Of the four idols of the heart, which one most often sabotages love in your life? How, specifically, does idolatry mess up your efforts to love others with Christ's love?
- How did it go yesterday, seeking to embrace and love "the one"? What is God specifically calling you to do? Share as much as is appropriate.

Additional Reading

Crazy Love by Francis Chan
Same Kind of Different as Me by Ron Hall and Denver Moore

Week 7
TRUST: LIVE THE BLANK

Day 1: Read—Chapter 6

- Read chapter 6 of *Sacred Mundane*. Highlight text and jot down your thoughts along the way so you'll be ready to discuss with your group.
- Write out Matthew 13:44 on a notecard. Review daily and commit to memory.

Day 2: Read—God's Goal for the World: His Kingdom Come

- Read again these well-known verses: John 3:16 and Matthew 28:18. What are God's feelings toward the world? What is his goal for it? How are we to be involved in this goal?
- Using Bible Gateway or another online concordance, do a word study of "the kingdom of God." There will be a lot of results! Take some time to read through these passages, jotting down any observations or things you learn. How would you explain the kingdom of God to someone else?
- Review Matthew 13:44.

Day 3: Reflect—Whose Kingdom?

- Are there any ways you can relate to my journey in the first half of chapter 6? In what ways has "don't mess up" become your default life goal? How has your own heart hunger trumped world hunger, leading you to constantly curve inward instead of living outward? How are you tempted to turn from seeking the kingdom of heaven to striving after the kingdom of self? Take a few moments today to honestly journal through your thoughts, asking God to reveal anything he wants to show you.
- Review Matthew 13:44.

Day 4: Read—Faith in the Face of Fear

- Read Genesis 22:1–19 and Mark 5:21–43. Try seeing the story through the eyes of Abraham and Jairus. What would you be feeling? How do God's commands seem impossible? How does his behavior not line up with what you might expect? What did Abraham and Jairus have to do in order to believe God and receive incredible blessing? What other characters in Scripture trusted in the face of fear?
- Review Matthew 13:44.

Day 5: Reflect—Confronting Your Fears

- In what area of your life are you most tempted to fear? Just between you and God, journal your greatest fear. Be honest with him about any ways that fear (of people, of death, of failure, of anything) creeps into your daily life and keeps you from trust. What are you holding on to tightly rather than letting go and trusting God? What would a completely fear-free life look like for you? How does fear cloud your decision-making, your relationships, and your ministry? Talk with God about the ways unhealthy fear holds you back, and ask him to show you how to partner with his Holy Spirit in moving forward in freedom. Consider doing a word study on fear in the Scriptures, asking God to banish it from your life.
- Review Matthew 13:44.

Day 6: Respond—Live the Blank

- What blank are you facing today? What dark unknown can you venture into by faith? Today, take a practical step of faith in this area, knowing that Jesus is with you. Make a date. Call that person. Outline a ministry plan. Research online. Make a financial commitment. Whatever God is calling you to do, obey him! Jot down your thoughts and make a specific plan for joyful, complete obedience.
- Review Matthew 13:44.

Day 7: Discussion

Today, as you gather with your group, we'll be discussing the following questions. Take a few moments now to look over this week's study and refresh your mind on what God has spoken to you and done in your heart.

- In what ways did you relate to my family's journey in this chapter? In what ways are you still seeking your own kingdom? How are you presently pursuing the hidden treasure in the field?
- Are there any ways your own life goals are merely "don't mess up"? Are you bound by "safe"? What heart hunger keeps you from noticing others' hunger? How can we pray for you in this area?
- As you feel comfortable responding, in what areas are you most prone to fear and are asking God to give you victory? What is the blank that feels unknown and scary—the place where you find it hard to trust? How can we pray for you?
- What would be most difficult to let go of?
- What practical step did you take yesterday in order to live the blank?

Additional Reading
The Hole in Our Gospel by Richard Stearns

Week 8
THANK: FIND FULFILLMENT

Day 1: Read—Chapter 7

- Read chapter 7 of *Sacred Mundane*. Highlight text and jot down your thoughts along the way so you'll be ready to discuss with your group.
- Write out Psalm 50:23 on a notecard. Review daily and commit to memory.

Day 2: Read—The God Who Disappoints

- Read Genesis 12:1–4; 21:5; Psalm 10. Meditate especially on Psalm 105:18–19. How did God disappoint these great men, then bring about glorious fulfillment for them in his own way? How does Joseph's statement in Genesis 50:20 capture the glorious truth that God deliberately allows disappointment to work glorious ends?
- Read John 11:1–44. Ask God to show you parallels in your own life, based on the discussion of expectations, disappointments, and fulfillment in this chapter.
- Review Psalm 50:23.

Day 3: Reflect—Identify Expectations, Disappointments, Fears

- In your journal, identify the top three things you are praying about (or just stewing about!) and hoping for. Be honest. Next to each item, write what you are expecting. That is, what would an answered prayer look like for you? Again, no extra points for super-spiritual answers. Honesty is all that counts.
- Next, write what stands out in your mind as disappointments in your life. You can list them or write them out, but consider the ways that God has allowed specific disappointment in your life. This is just between you and God.

- Then, identify any fears that have resulted from those disappointments and perhaps influenced your current expectations. Write any current fears that come to mind. What connections do you see between your fears and your expectations?
- Review Psalm 50:23.

Day 4: Read—Expectancy Without Expectation

- Reread 2 Kings 5:1–17. Enter back into this story, considering all we have learned about disappointment and fulfillment. In your own words, how did God disappoint Naaman in order to do something infinitely greater instead?
- Reread Romans 5:3–5 and Psalms 42:11, 43:5, and 62:5. How would you explain to another person what true hope is?
- Read Psalm 66:10–12. What pattern does this passage outline in terms of how God often deals with his people?
- Review Psalm 50:23.

Day 5: Reflect—The Two Cycles

- Review the two cycles: Fear ➛ Expectation ➛ Disappointment and Faith ➛ Expectancy ➛ Fulfillment. Where have you experienced these cycles in your life? Ask God to help you identify where you are on the disappointment cycle. How can you choose the off-ramp of thanksgiving, letting go of expectation in exchange for true faith, trusting him even when you cannot see? Ask him to translate this process for whatever issue or circumstance you are facing today. Be specific.
- Review Psalm 50:23.

Day 6: Respond—Bring It All Together (LET)

- On one piece of paper write out what we have processed so far.
  - ✱ How does the sentence of your life read right now? What is the *but* where you are wanting to see God move?
  - ✱ Flesh out where you need to *let* him in. Finish this statement:

"I want Jesus to come transform my _____."
Journal how you believe God is calling you to more fully
surrender the lordship of your life to him in this area. Be specific.

* Write a sentence describing how you see this situation through
the lens of God's Word. When you *look* at it through God's eyes,
what is the real issue? Jot down any key verses that help you
further define or clarify the situation.

* Identify anything you have discerned God showing you in
prayer regarding this issue. Or perhaps the insight here is that
you haven't prayed about it. Start there. If you have been praying
about it, what do you sense the Spirit impressing on your heart?
Make sure that what you are hearing lines up with the truth of
Scripture.

* Next, write a sentence explaining how you will engage and enter
into the nitty gritty of your daily interaction with this situation.
How will you refuse to give up, pull back, or check out? This will
widely vary based on the circumstance, but identify any way you
will be purposeful not to escape, but to *let* this challenge work
hupomone into your heart.

* Write the name of "the one" whom God is calling you to embrace. It may be directly or indirectly related to the issue at
hand, but everything is connected, so it all matters. After the
name, write in one sentence how you will specifically embrace
this person with practical and sacrificial love.

* Write a sentence saying what it will look like for you to forsake
fear and *trust* God with this issue. What does "living the blank"
look like in this situation? Again, be as specific as possible.

* Summarize your current expectation (from day 3) for this situation, and any fears that may be fueling this expectation. Write
a sentence describing what it would mean to live in expectancy
instead, trusting God with this situation completely, waiting for
him, having true hope. Then list five to ten things for which you
are truly thankful.

* Finally, plan a time with a close friend or spouse when you will
share this page, asking for prayer, wisdom, and accountability.
- Review Psalm 50:23.

Day 7: Discussion

Today, as your group convenes, share with each other—to the extent
each of you is comfortable—your "Bring It All Together (LET)" results
from yesterday. Ask questions and help one another process. Pray for one
another, asking for God's insight, wisdom, and power in each specific
situation.

Additional Reading

Inside Out by Dr. Larry Crabb

Week 9
LET YOUR LIFE BE POURED OUT

Day 1: Read—Chapter 8
- Read chapter 8 of *Sacred Mundane*. Highlight text and jot down your thoughts along the way so you'll be ready to discuss with your group.
- Write out Isaiah 58:10 on a notecard. Review daily and commit to memory.

Day 2: Read—Poured Out
- Read Mark 12:41–44; 14:3–9; Philippians 2:17; 2 Timothy 4:6. What do you learn from these examples of being poured out? What strikes you most from their example? From what you read and what you know about the lives of these Bible characters, what obstacles did they face? Why would their offerings have been challenging to them? How do you identify with them?
- Review Isaiah 58:10.

Day 3: Reflect—Spiritual Self-Improvement
- Do you see any ways that your efforts at growing may be forms of spiritual self-improvement instead of pure devotion to Christ? How so? What selfish motivation most easily creeps in and corrupts your efforts to follow Jesus?
- How can this change? Take some time today to talk to God and journal your thoughts, honestly evaluating whether you are ready to offer your life fully to him, to be poured out and to be "picked" as he wishes.
- Review Isaiah 58:10.

Day 4: Read—Wholehearted Worship
- Read Isaiah 58 and Malachi 1:6–9, 13–14; 3:8–10. What critique

does God give his people in each of these situations? How were they offering him less than their best? How was it a halfhearted, not wholehearted, offering? What, specifically, were they doing—or not doing? How could that habit be translated into modern-day terms? Conversely, what does God promise to do if they change their ways and pour out their lives in wholehearted worship? What are the specific promises? Write them down. These are precious promises for those who will follow Jesus completely. Take hold of them!

- Review Isaiah 58:10.

Day 5: Reflect—Last Days

- How does it strike you that these are the last days? Are you fearful? Excited? A bit nervous? A mix of all three? If Jesus were to return, say, in the next year, how would it impact your daily life? What changes would you make in your mundane? How would it affect your goals, dreams, vision? How does a sense of urgency, of time being short, impact your choices today?
- Review Isaiah 58:10.

Day 6: Respond—Climb Up on the Altar

- Reread Oswald Chambers's words on page 169. Are you ready to offer your life as a poured-out drink offering? Are there ways you are tempted to hold back certain areas, calculating and divvying up your life and only offering certain parts? What comes to mind when you consider what area may still be tucked away, hidden, untouched by his transforming hand? Take time today, as long as it takes, to get real with God and ask him to help you surrender all areas to him. Consider the words of the beautiful hymn "Take My Life," and ask him to let that be true in your life. Journal your thoughts, reservations, fears. Give them to him. Let this be a day of decision in your life.
- How will you "tie yourself" to this decision? Whom will you tell?

What things can you set in place to help make this happen? What can you cut off, cancel, or get rid of? Or what can you add, subscribe to, or bring in? What will help you go the way of Jesus?

- Review Isaiah 58:10.

Day 7: Discussion

Today as you gather, share how God is calling you to *let* your life be poured out.

- What struck you from the lives of Paul, the woman with the flask of oil, and the widow with her mites? How are you tempted to only give part of your life over to God? How can you freely and fully pour out everything to him instead?
- Where in your life do you see evidence of spiritual self-improvement instead of true worship?
- How would the issues discussed in Malachi and Isaiah 58 be translated to our world today? In what ways do we offer God less than our best or use spiritual activity as a means of getting what we want?
- How does it strike you that Christ is returning soon?
- Are you ready to be poured out as a drink offering? How will you tie yourself to the altar? How can the rest of the group help tie you down? How can they provide helpful, loving, supportive accountability? Now that this study is over, what is your plan for moving forward, helping each other remain on the altar, continually pouring out your lives as a living sacrifice? Be as specific as possible. Make a plan for continuing to meet together, or break into twos or threes. Continue on your Bible reading plan, or begin one today. Read the recommended books listed at the bottom of each week's study. This week's recommendations are especially powerful for seeing what God can do through people who poured out their lives for the sake of the world. Finish your time by praying for each other, asking for God to continue his good work in and through each of your lives.

Additional Reading

Rees Howells, Intercessor by Norman Grubb

The Heavenly Man by Brother Yun

The Jesus Fast by Lou Engle

Notes

Chapter 1: LET Him In

1. Her name has been changed to protect my dear friend's privacy.
2. C. S. Lewis, *Mere Christianity* (New York: Simon & Schuster, 1996), 56.
3. Brother Lawrence, *The Practice of the Presence of God* (New Kensington, PA: Whitaker House, 1982), 45.
4. Ibid., 20.
5. William Barclay, *The Letters to the Philippians, Colossians, and Thessalonians* (Edinburgh: Saint Andrew Press, 1959), 131.

Chapter 2: LOOK: See the World Through the Word

1. Dietrich Bonhoeffer, *Life Together* (New York: Harper & Row, 1954), 83.
2. Jean Pierre de Caussade, *The Sacrament of the Present Moment* (Scotts Valley, CA: CreateSpace Independent Publishing, 2013), 80.
3. A. W. Tozer, *The Pursuit of God* (Camp Hill, PA: Christian Publications, 1982), 95.
4. I wholeheartedly recommend *Women of the Word: How to Study the Bible with Both Our Hearts and Minds* by Jen Wilkin (Wheaton, IL: Crossway, 2014) as a starting point for your personal Bible study.

Chapter 3: LISTEN: Discern His Voice in Daily Life

1. This is perfectly portrayed in Philippians 2:5–8: Jesus is identified as fully a son but is offering himself as a slave for the sake of reaching us. We are told to have the same mind-set as this.
2. Paul Miller, *A Praying Life: Connecting with God in a Distracting World* (Colorado Springs: NavPress, 2009), 33.

3. William Barclay, *The Letters to the Philippians, Colossians, and Thessalonians* (Edinburgh: Saint Andrew Press, 1959), 131.

4. Ibid., 132.

Chapter 4: ENGAGE: Enter In

1. A. W. Tozer, *The Pursuit of God* (Camp Hill, PA: Christian Publications, 1982), 127.

2. Abraham Kuyper, inaugural lecture, Free University of Amsterdam, 1880.

3. Tozer, *The Pursuit of God*, 117.

4. Ibid., 119.

5. Kathleen Norris, *The Quotidian Mysteries: Laundry, Liturgy and "Women's Work"* (Mahwah, NJ: Paulist Press, 1998), 4.

Chapter 5: EMBRACE: Love the One

1. C. S. Lewis, *The Weight of Glory* (New York: HarperOne, 2001), 45–46.

2. C. S. Lewis, quoted in John R. W. Stott, *The Epistles of John* (Grand Rapids: Eerdmans, 1964), 143.

3. John Calvin, *Institutes of the Christian Religion* (Peabody, MA: Hendrickson, 2008), 1.11.8, 55.

4. Caesar Kalinowski, *The Gospel Primer* (Littleton, CO: Missio Publishing, 2013), 115.

Chapter 6: TRUST: Live the Blank

1. A. W. Tozer, *The Pursuit of God* (Camp Hill, PA: Christian Publications, 1982), 21. Tozer highlights the blessed state of absolute surrender, when nothing threatens the holy throne of our hearts where God alone dwells.

2. Ibid., 22.

Chapter 8: LET Your Life Be Poured Out

1. C. S. Lewis, *Letters of C. S. Lewis*, ed. W. H. Lewis (New York: Harcourt, Brace & World, 1966), 256.

2. Oswald Chambers, "Are You Ready to Be Poured Out as an Offering? (2)" *My Utmost for His Highest*, http://utmost.org/are-you-ready-to-be-poured-out-as-an-offering-2/. Emphasis mine.

About the Author

—————◆—————◆—————

KARI PATTERSON IS A beloved daughter of God, and her life's aim is to please her Father. She is married to Pastor Jeff, and together they are raising two quirky kiddos and lead a Christ-centered community called Renew Church. Kari holds a master's degree in pastoral studies from Multnomah Seminary, speaks at women's events, and writes at karipatterson.com. She loves the smell of fresh-baked bread and her children's morning-breath. #sacredmundane

Let's Connect!
Website: karipatterson.com
Facebook: @sacredmundane
Twitter: @karipatterson
Instagram: @karipatterson

Kari would love to hear from you! Please feel free to email questions, comments, or stories through her website. Be sure to #sacredmundane on social media shares so we can all celebrate life's messy glory together!

Invite Kari to Your Event!
Check out karipatterson.com/speaking for more information on inviting Kari to speak at your event. She has a wide variety of topics and options available, including a *Sacred Mundane* weekend retreat, day event, or one-time workshop.